Humane approach to urban planning

Other titles of interest:

Smart Urban and Rural Planning Techniques
Harmit Singh Bedi

Fixing flawed urban planning: The case of Delhi
Boniface G. Fernandes

Geographic Information System for Smart Cities
Prof. TM Vinod Kumar and Associates

Metropolitan Governance: Cases of Ahmedabad and Hyderabad
Dr. Vinita Yadav

India's Urban Confusion: Challenges and Strategies
Edited by Dr. M. Ramachandran

Designing Better Architecture Education: Global Realities and Local Reforms
Dr Manjari Chakraborty

The Ekistics of Animal and Human Conflict
Rishi Dev

Water Conservation Techniques in Traditional Human Settlements
Pietro Laureano

The City Observed: Notes from an Unfolding India
Pallavi Shrivastava

Tirtha at Mukteswar: Architecture and Documentation
Dr. Ranjana Mital and Prabhjot Singh Sugga

Humane approach to urban planning

Priya Choudhary

COPAL PUBLISHING GROUP
Inspiring for a better future through publishing

Published by Copal Publishing Group
E-143, Lajpat Nagar, Sahibabad,
Distt. Ghaziabad, UP – 201005, India

www.copalpublishing.com

First Published 2015
© Copal Publishing Group, 2015

This book contains information obtained from authentic and highly regarded sources. Reprinted material is quoted with permission. Reasonable efforts have been made to publish reliable data and information, but the authors and the publishers cannot assume responsibility for the validity of all materials. Neither the authors nor the publishers, nor anyone else associated with this publication, shall be liable for any loss, damage or liability directly or indirectly caused or alleged to be caused by this book.

Neither this book nor any part may be reproduced or transmitted in any form or by any means, electronic or mechanical, including photocopying, microfilming and recording, or by any information storage or retrieval system, without permission in writing from Copal Publishing Group. The consent of Copal Publishing Group does not extend to copying for general distribution, for promotion, for creating new works, or for resale. Specific permission must be obtained in writing from Copal Publishing Group for such copying.

Trademark notice: Product or corporate names may be trademarks or registered trademarks, and are used only for identification and explanation, without intent to infringe.

ISBN: 978-93-83419-21-0 (hard back)
ISBN: 978-93-83419-22-7 (e-book)

Typeset by Bhumi Graphics, New Delhi
Printed and bound by Bhavish Graphics, Chennai

Contents

Preface	ix
Foreword	xi
Acknowledgments	xiii
List of figures	xv
List of tables	xix

1. Introduction — 1
  1.1 Prologue — 4
  1.2 Man and built environment relationship — 12
  1.3 Spatial cognition — 13
  1.4 Cognitive approach — 15
  1.5 References — 17

2. Urbanisation and urbanism in India — 19
  2.1 Urbanisation and urbanism — 22
  2.2 Contemporary planning practices — 23
  2.3 User preferences — 25
  2.4 References — 27

3. Spatial configuration and cognition — 29
  3.1 Epistemological basis — 32
  3.2 Comprehension of user preferences — 41
  3.3 Spatial configuration — 43
  3.4 Configuration: Socio-cultural implications — 45

3.5	Spatial configuration: Past, present and future	51
3.6	Concept of depth	55
3.7	Spatial cognition	69
3.8	Cognitive mapping	71
3.9	Syntactic analysis for cognition studies	79
3.10	Indian context	82
3.11	Spatial design	85
3.12	Summary	86

4. User preferences and traditional Indian settlements   89

4.1	Significance	92
4.2	Traditional built environments	93
4.3	Procedure	101
4.4	Analysis	102
4.5	Numerical synthesis	107
4.6	Traditional settlements – configurational peculiarities	113
4.7	References	113

5. User preferences in contemporary cities   115

5.1	Nagpur: Evolution	118
5.2	Syntactic analysis of Nagpur	120
5.3	Select localities: Syntactic properties	129
5.4	Select localities: Mahal and Trimurti Nagar	130
5.5	Methodology	133
5.6	Observations and analysis	137

5.7	Configurational peculiarity and user preferences	148
5.8	Summary	155
5.9	References	156

6. Principles of urbanism for Indian cities — 157

6.1	Planning practices: Euclidian geometry	160
6.2	Principles of urbanism	161
6.3	References	166

7. Humane approach for planning practices — 167

7.1	Humane approach	170
7.2	Proposed spatial modelling	171
7.3	Reforms for urban planning practices	173
7.4	References	175

Preface

Development plans are prepared intermittently for all cities in India. Developments take place but at the same time, many proposals fail; and it is realized that there is a mismatch between what citizens want and what is provided. There is a need to look at the whole issue of planning from users' perspective. The planning approach followed mostly ignores the cultural peculiarities, habits, preferences of Indian users. The work done in building good cities under city planning is no way to be discredited or discounted for its effectiveness. However, it may be useful to move ahead and incorporate culture-specific user aspects and evolve a humane approach to city planning in India.

Being a user of the city and a planner-designer myself, there were few observations. The way we – the planners – plan roads, open spaces, locations for markets, institutes and other important public spaces; at times does not match the way users tend to use them. The spaces planned for traffic and transportation are used for interactions, religious political events, processions and sports. It leads to lot of conflicting situations. It is also realized that my preferences as a user are not as logical and legitimate as the way I think, describe or plan built environments. This is mainly because all the city planning and preparation of development plans is based on the planning norms formulated in Europe or North America. We grossly follow them without understanding its appropriateness in to the Indian situations. Due to socio-economic, demographic and cultural differences in Indian context, the Indian users and their preferences are very much different. The planning approach without understanding appropriately the Indian context and Indian users grossly fails. There are lot of physical and social implications such as environmental and socio-cultural conflicts. Illegal developments and encroachments emerge. The way users behave and life gets emerged in cities can be defined as urbanism. Thus one can define the major problem for planning and planners is that perhaps there is a mismatch between culture-specific Indian principles of urbanism and the principles of urbanism followed as planning norms.

There is a detailed study done by the author about user preferences by understanding the way users structure spaces around in their mind and then use. It brought out few facts about the peculiarities of Indian users, their preferences and Indian principles of urbanism, which are discussed in the book.

The old part of the city or traditional built environments may have many problems, but as living environments they appear to be much more humane and cohesive. These built environments evolved gradually as per the user preferences. With the accelerated pace of urbanization, many such small- and medium-size cities are rapidly growing. If growth is not managed properly at this moment of rapid urbanization, it can be disastrous. Moreover, with the open market economy, cities are planned and designed so as to be marketed. But one should not forget that cities are living environments. Especially the way neighborhoods, the prime living environments, are dealt by planners and designers have lot of implications not just on the physical environment but the social environment as well. Thus consideration of user preferences will not only reduce conflicting situations in urban areas due to non-congruence between planning principles adopted and principles of urbanism rooted in the place, but will also help to develop living social environments in developing cities.

Priya Choudhary

Foreword

I am pleased to present a book by Priya Sameer Choudhary titled "Humane Approach to Urban Planning" which is consequential result of her meticulous doctoral research work. I am further ecstatic to express my thoughts, not since Priya is amongst the foremost doctoral degree awardees under my guidance, but primarily because of the extensive, exclusive, and exquisitely gratifying research that she has carried out.

One of the difficulty commonly observed while identifying problems involving urban issues is losing sight of its most vital component that is human beings. This is even truer while we attempt making claims for better development initiatives in an urban setting as we have it in Indian cities. Architects and planners have a great role to play in improving not only the physical environment but also the socio-cultural environment in the cities. For example, in a diverse country like India, where socio-cultural environments are varied and sensitive, points out that, planners need to adapt themselves to its indigenous target group and its needs.

There are acts, control-oriented planning practices and intricate processes; yet, the desired effect and appropriateness of planning interventions is calling for a major shift. Therefore, it is of paramount importance that the decision makers should resort to methods and techniques like, syntactic analysis when dealing with built environments.

Priya Choudhary has demonstrated precisely, through this study, how choices and preferences of a native user linked to cultural settings of Indian type could open a new dimension of approach for the architects and planners. The book uses an important tool to measure the *'Indianness'* that bring out stunning facts about the characteristic peculiarities of Indian users, their preferences, which in turn, kick off the demand to evolve India-specific urbanism principles and approach to embark upon. *The serious concern to identify 'Indianness' in existing built environments and possible amends to make in present planning practices has lead the author to initiate this work.* This revelation is I believe a major contribution that the book has made. It is pertinent and logical that the book further evolves a working framework for decision makers and role players involved in spatial planning to integrate such a humane approach while dealing with continuously evolving built environments in Urban India.

The book marks the beginning of a sojourn on an identified promising path and challenges the young researchers may continue to trot by choice. It could lead to rational understanding for the key urban issues such as encroachments and illegal developments in Indian cities. It therefore possible to address queries like: Where we go wrong? What are the loopholes? Can we create India-specific planning norms/ methods? Thus, the book has made a profound contribution by establishing the need to evolve a humane approach in the existing planning practices. Scholars, professionals can hold the thread from it and stretch it further to mark a positive impact as they deem fit.

Dr. Vinayak S. Adane
Professor
Department of Architecture and Planning,
VNIT, Nagpur

Acknowledgments

The doctoral research by me titled, 'A cognitive approach to spatial modelling of built environments in urban India' has formed the basis for the book. I would like to acknowledge the support of all the teaching and non-teaching staff members of Visveswaraya National Institute of technology (VNIT) who allowed me to undertake the intended research and extended required assistance and guidance from time to time. I am grateful to my guide Dr. Vinayak Adane for the valuable guidance, caring support and encouragement. His confidence in me and positive criticism helped me to complete my doctoral research which eventually led to the formation of the book. The guidance and support from Dr. Alpana Dongre and Dr. Rahul Ralegaonkar was equally important. I appreciate the cooperation and inspiration extended by them.

Many organizations and institutions have supported me in this endeavor with great patience. During the research, I was selected for Fulbright Nehru Doctoral and Professional research fellowship. I find myself very privileged as noted contemporary architecture historian Prof. Nezar Al Sayyad from Centre for Environmental Design and Research, University of California, Berkeley, accepted me as a student during my tenure as a Fulbright scholar. A positive dialogue with him shaped my research ideas appropriately. I am thankful to Fulbright commission in India, New Delhi, and its senior staff members, for giving me this opportunity and also helping me out with the modalities throughout.

This is all possible because the Institution in which I work, Women's Education Society's Smt. Manoramabai Mundle College of Architecture, allowed me to take up the research and its publication. I highly appreciate the support of Director and Secretary of WES, Dr. Panna Akhani, and Principal of the institution, Dr. Ujwala Chakradeo. The indirect and direct guidance, support and encouragement of all my colleagues are equally important.

Dr. Vrinda Joglekar, Head of the Department of Statistics, Hislop college, Nagpur, helped me immensely in statistical analysis; and I would like to confess that without her contribution, this wouldn't have been possible.

Finally, I am grateful to my family and friends for their time-to-time support, help and encouragement, without which the completion of this project was impossible.

Priya S. Choudhary

List of Figures

Chapter 1	**Introduction**
Figure 1.1	System of spaces in old Nagpur
Figure 1.2	Determinants of built environment
Figure 1.3	Intense interactions between users and built environment
Figure 1.4	Users modify buildings as per the needs
Figure 1.5	Spatial experience
Figure 1.6	Relationship: Spatial configuration and spatial cognition
Figure 1.7	Investigation approach
Chapter 2	**Urbanisation and urbanism in India**
Figure 2.1	Plan process
Figure 2.2	Temple, hawkers on the street …order imposed by users
Chapter 3	**Spatial configuration and cognition**
Figure 3.1	Development of spatial cognition
Figure 3.2	Neighbourhood in Bay Area near San Francisco
Figure 3.3	Spectrum of theories related to user–built environment relationship
Figure 3.4	Gradual transformation of a gridded Roman colony into an Islamic city
Figure 3.5	Convex and axial space
Figure 3.6	Permeability graphs of lines 3 and 2
Figure 3.7	Axial lines in curved spaces

Figure 3.8	Axial map: Process
Figure 3.9	Axial map: Errors
Figure 3.10	Permeability graphs of Lines 1 and 4
Figure 3.11	Shifting axis of movement
Figure 3.12	Use of street for religious, social, political or commercial activities
Figure 3.13	System of spaces and axial map
Figure 3.14	Axial map
Chapter 4	**User preferences and traditional Indian settlements**
Figure 4.1	Spatial configuration: Traditional urban core (Varanasi)
Figure 4.2	Map of India with selected cities
Figure 4.3	Bhopal: Core area
Figure 4.4	Lucknow: Core area
Figure 4.5	Varanasi: Core area
Figure 4.6	Nashik: Core area
Figure 4.7	Nagpur: Core area
Figure 4.8	Integration (Rn) map of urban core (Mahal) of Nagpur
Figure 4.9	Integration (Rn) map of urban core of Bhopal
Figure 4.10	Integration (Rn) map of urban core of Nashik
Figure 4.11	Integration (Rn) map of urban core of Lucknow
Figure 4.12	Integration (Rn) map of urban core of Varanasi
Figure 4.13	Integration (Rn) map of Chandigarh
Figure 4.14	Relationship between number of axes and area
Figure 4.15	Synergy and intelligibility of Chandigarh in comparison to traditional Indian urban cores

Figure 4.16	Traditional urban cores: Syntactic parameters
Figure 4.17	Syntactic parameters: Indian and other built environments
Figure 4.18	Synergy and intelligibility: Comparison
Chapter 5	**User preferences in contemporary cities**
Figure 5.1	Nagpur: Settlement evolution
Figure 5.2	Map of Nagpur
Figure 5.3	Scattergrams: Intelligibility and synergy of Nagpur
Figure 5.4	Scattergrams: Intelligibility and synergy of traditional core of Nagpur
Figure 5.5	Query result of value 'Integration (HH)'>0.85
Figure 5.6	Query result of value 'Integration (HH)'>0.75
Figure 5.7	Proposed land-use plan of Dhantoli and Sitabuldi
Figure 5.8	Result of query: Value 'Integration (HH) R3' > 3.5
Figure 5.9	Proposed land-use plan of West Nagpur
Figure 5.10	Festive celebrations on West High Court Road
Figure 5.11	Chor Bazar and its configurational peculiarity
Figures 5.12	Location of installation of community Ganpati/Durga idol: Gopal Nagar and Madhav Nagar
Figures 5.13	Local integration maps: Gopal and Madhav Nagar
Figure 5.14	Selected localities
Figure 5.15	Google image: Mahal
Figure 5.16	Close knit, organically evolved urban fabric in Mahal
Figure 5.17	Google image: Trimurti Nagar
Figure 5.18	Grid-iron pattern of Trimurti Nagar
Figure 5.19	'Appealing buildings' mentioned by the respondents in new planned area (Trimurti Nagar)

Figure 5.20	'Appealing buildings' mentioned by the respondents in Mahal
Figure 5.21	Global integration (Rn) map of Mahal: Smaller but many axes
Figure 5.22	Global integration (Rn) map of Trimurti Nagar: Longer and fewer axes
Figure 5.23	Local integration map of Mahal
Figure 5.24	Local integration map of Trimurti Nagar
Figure 5.25	Social activities on internal streets of Mahal
Figure 5.26	Defined open spaces in Trimurti Nagar
Figure 5.27	Local integration map and immergence of activity node: Gopal Nagar
Figure 5.28	Local integration map of Saraswati Vihar
Chapter 6	**Principles of urbanism for Indian cities**
Figure 6.1	Evolved social space
Figure 6.2	Commercial developments on highly accessible movement corridors
Figure 6.3	Urban neighbourhood
Figure 6.4	Streets as social space
Figure 6.5	Visibility of facilities
Chapter 7	**Humane approach for planning practices** 167
Figure 7.1	Proposed spatial modelling
Figure 7.2	Applicability in general plan process

List of Tables

Chapter 3	**Spatial configuration and cognition**	**29**
Table 3.1	Syntactic measures	66
Table 3.2	Parameters	69
Chapter 4	**User preferences and traditional Indian settlements**	**89**
Table 4.1	Number of axes	107
Table 4.2	Syntactic parameters: Traditional cities and Chandigarh	110
Table 4.3	Syntactic parameters: World scenario	112
Chapter 5	**User preferences in contemporary cities**	**115**
Table 5.1	Syntactic parameters of Nagpur	121
Table 5.2	Syntactic analysis of identified localities	130
Table 5.3	Matrix of parameters and methods	134
Table 5.4	Correlation Matrix: Syntactic parameters and frequency of use	137
Table 5.5	Correlation Matrix: Syntactic parameters and frequency of recognition	140
Table 5.6	Indices of use of global and local facilities	144
Table 5.7	Indices of recognition	145

Chapter 1

Photo: Sitabuldi Main Road, Nagpur

Chapter 1
Introduction

Abstract: This chapter discusses the background of the need of understanding and incorporating human aspects of urban planning practices in India. After the independence, these are emerging on the basis of the planning norms based on Western European or North American experiences. Yet, Indian built environments and users interact in a peculiar manner. The understanding of the cognitive constructs as per user preferences through the study of relationship of spatial cognition and spatial configuration can help us to understand the principles of urbanism in Indian context. This understanding can help planners and designers while dealing emerging built environments in urban area.

Key words: Built environment, spatial cognition, spatial configuration, urbanism

1.1 Prologue

India is in a rapid phase of urbanization. Up till now, the urbanization process was mainly affecting megacities; but now the small and medium cities are also developing. The physical organization and design of cities has taken an inflated role in the world economy (Cuthbert, 2003). Same is the case with many developing Indian cities.

In India, most of the issues related to built environment are still dealt with the approach based on the realm of urban planning. The built environments in post-independence India are emerging on the basis of the planning norms formulated in relation to the modern industrial cities developed in Europe or North America. The patterns of new spatial configurations based on 'urban rationality' are being grossly applied to existing built environments or developing new built environments in India, without actually understanding its appropriateness to the Indian situations. Due to socio-economic, demographic and cultural differences in Indian context, the evolving built environments have lot of physical and social implications such as environmental and socio-cultural conflicts. The approach to deal urban built environments mostly ignored the human aspects of built environment and focused on the logic of 'good environmental quality' in terms of transportation and health considerations. The work done in building up good cities under city planning or urban planning is no way to be discredited or discounted for its effectiveness. However, it may be useful to move ahead and incorporate culture-specific user aspects. Hence there is a need to understand the peculiarities of spatial organization in Indian context and the reasons for it, and evolve a humane approach to deal emerging built environments in urban India.

1.1.1 Built environment

Built environments basically mean everything that is humanely created, modified, arranged or maintained. Thus, collectively, the products and processes of human creation are called the built environment (McClure, Bartuska, and Bartuska, 2007, p.5). Another definition by Clarke (2003) states that built environment is a simplistic title of credible utility, for a complex assemblage of various constructions each produced within specific conditions and various regulatory and financial structures. It is as old as mankind. Yet, 'built environment' is a relatively recent and very much inclusive concept. We have been studying and analyzing built environment under the heads such as architecture, urban design, urban planning, etc. Understanding 'built environment' as all inclusive concept makes a lot of difference. The focus is on the interrelationships between man and environment.

There are many determinants of the form of a built environment. It is a resultant of many forces or determinants interacting in a diverse manner through space and time (Batty and Longley, 1994). Kostof (1993) referred to three interlocking elements of built environment, which are initially described by M.R.G. Conzen. They are street pattern, land-use pattern and building fabric defining the city in three dimensions.

Thus built environments can be defined as organization of space, as they consist of space (unbuilt) and matter (built). In a built environment, the spaces are linked to each other, forming a 'system of spaces'. Such system of spaces in old Nagpur is shown in Fig. 1.1. The way these individual spaces are formed and most importantly linked together is responsible for spatial configuration of the built environment.

Figure 1.1 System of spaces in old Nagpur

The determinants of urban form listed by Kostof (1993) include topography, synoecism, land division processes and social orders. Topography means natural setting, which certainly affects the urban form. Synoecism means administrative setup and arrangements, that govern processes of land division. These are physical determinants but the response to them is obviously in accordance to social structure, order and limits of social control due to peculiarities of culture and ethnicity. Thus the three important determinants of the spatial configuration in a built environment are as follows: firstly, natural setting in terms of topography, climate; secondly, political and bureaucratic setup; and thirdly, human response to these contextual aspects. These are shown in Fig. 1.2. Throughout the world, the natural settings remaining similar, the built environments differ; predominantly due to user preferences and values. Modern spatial organization is usually given functionalist and economic explanations yet the morphological prototypes of the new urban areas were developed 50 years before the invention of motor car (Hillier and Hanson, 1984). This proves that underlying principle of spatial configurations in a built environment is predominantly based on human or to be specific, user response. This aspect or determinant of built environment has been largely ignored in contemporary practices of dealing built environments.

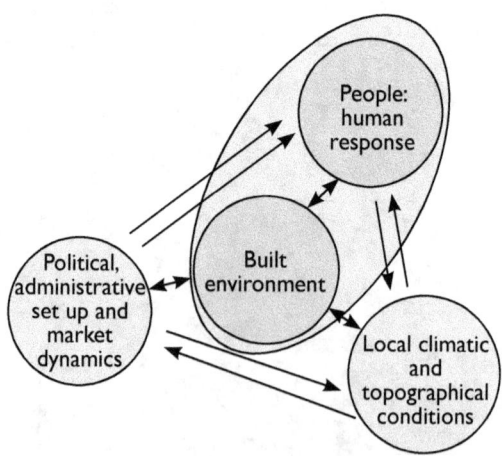

Figure 1.2 Determinants of built environment

The physical configuration in a built environment and social environment are two sides of same coin and that is the 'system of spaces'. They are very much related and one affects the other. Physical form of the built environment has an effect on social environment; and over a period, social environment shapes the built environment. It's a cyclic process, and changing quality of spatial configurations is responsible for changing social life and vice versa. Sir Winston Churchill (1924) has commented about the social implications of built environment as, 'We shape buildings and thereafter they shape us' (Lockton, 2011). Systematizing of space, in turn, provides a framework for the desired social intercourse in any settlement. So spatial systems not only are a result of but also provide a guide to the convention of behaviour and civil conduct for any society at a particular time (Kumar, 1998).

The planners are responsible for shaping the spatial configuration of the built environment, which affects the social environment as well; hence, there is a need for understanding configuration. Lack of understanding of the precise nature of the relation between spatial configuration and social life is the chief obstacle to better design of built environments (Hillier and Hanson, 1984). Hence for ensuring better design and planning decision strategy for built environments, there is a need to understand and quantify spatial configuration and its effect on social environment.

Various forms of built environments exist in India, as India is a vast country with a lot of geographic, climatic, ethnic, religious and linguistic diversity. It has a history full of intense, political and cultural experiences. Therefore it has multiple and pluralistic manifestations, resulting in multilayered built environments (Desai, 2007). Another important aspect about Indian built environment is that India's built heritage does not confine to historic preserved objects frozen in their own time and space, but rather as cultural traditions, which have transcended the time and space to remain alive and appropriate even in the present (Pandya, 2004). Thus, in India we simultaneously live in three time zones. Legacies of past and aspirations for the future effectively combine with the realities of present. Till date, the Indian built environments have been very much 'living' and 'thus 'evolving'. Figure 1.3 shows intense interactions between users and built environment.

Figure 1.3 Intense interactions between users and built environment

1.1.2 Humane aspects of built environment

Traditionally, not only in India but in most of the world, built environments evolved gradually and values about user preferences got embedded into it. This acted as a regulator or controller of its progression (Rapoport, 1969). In absence of any municipal authorities, the force of tradition and consolidated social order supervised the city forms (Kostof, 1993). The new value system based on urban planning principles was accepted in post-industrial revolution period and in case of India, post-independence period. It neglected the culture-specific user preferences. At times, planners/designers and the public represent very different value systems (Rapoport, 1977). Rapoport (1977) has extensively discussed the role of culture-specific values, role of spatial configuration and the way people perceive, cognize and then use the built environments. The non-congruence between the designers' norms and users' requirements of spaces are discussed in depth by him. For planners, the traditionally evolved built environments with organic spatial configuration are usually chaotic due to obvious geometric irregularity which is considered as 'disorder'(Karimi, 1997). Yet, the spatial configurations of traditional built environments seem quite in harmony with the users, as there are fewer conflicts between built environments and its users. These environments are found to be much more 'humane' because of the congruence between user preferences and its configuration. The spatial configurations in contemporary built environments resulting out of the rational ordering of space have gradually disowned the 'organic order' in traditionally evolved built environment in India. Built environments that exist today in India are very complex environments with influences from number of periods as per the process of natural selection.

This does not mean that there is a need to return to the past. Nevertheless, there is a need to evolve a methodological framework by which culture-specific user preferences can be understood. It can contribute in making the plan process for dealing the urban environments much more context specific and help in making built environments much more humane. Thus, there is a need for understanding user preferences while dealing urban environments.

User preferences if not taken care of appropriately while dealing built environment, one can find emergence of conflicting built environment due to a tussle between designed spatial configuration and its use. Cities are not only made up of the structures in which urban functions are located and where people perform their daily activities, but also made up of the people who live in the structures give life to this objective form by means of daily activities. Same is true about the buildings as well. Designers design the buildings irrespective of user preferences; and hence, we find that users modify it as per the needs. Figure 1.4 shows an example of residential apartment, where users have imposed their own order by personalized treatments to individual balconies.

Figure 1.4 Users modify buildings as per the needs

The discussions about contemporary built environments throughout the world have highlighted a need to develop a scientific approach to the built environment through environment behavior investigation. Planners or designers, till very recently, followed an approach based on normative theories about 'what it should be'

(Hillier, 1996). There is a need to develop a lot of positive theories which can help us to understand the built environments as they are and the way they are evolving. Also the reasons as to 'why' they are evolving in that manner. There is a need for Indian built environment studies contributing to positive theories. This is almost similar to Alexander's thesis (1964) in which he argues that good design or good decision making in a broader sense must be based on an understanding of the ways the system evolves through the elements within its hierarchy (Batty and Longley, 1994).

The interventions in the city can only be based on the understanding of the city. If the understanding is deficit, the effects are destructive. The value system according to which we have been transforming our cities over the past century has always appeared as a kind of urban rationality, but never based on the study of the city (Hillier, 1996). Stressing the similar need, Rapoport (1992) has mentioned in an interview that in other fields, people test their intuitions before they use them or make them public. The broader the sample for study of built environments – in space and in time – the more likely we are able to see regularities in apparent chaos and to understand better the significant differences, i.e. the more likely we are to see patterns and relationships (Rapoport, 1979). This means there is a need to study many cases of built environments to understand better in terms of peculiarities and the reasons for it.

The knowledge base in regards to built environment design should evolve from many other disciplines including cognitive science, artificial intelligence, scientific methods, logic and mathematics. Investigation needs to be interdisciplinary and should aim at synthesis of lot of empirical studies done. The purpose of synthesis is to boil down theories to few principles which can become basis for applications in design. The methodological framework on the basis of synthesis of number of theories can help planners and designers to identify user preferences of a society under consideration appropriately, before they can indulge into planning/design tasks. To understand user preferences, the man–built-environment interface needs to be focused.

1.2 Man and built environment relationship

The man and built environment relationship is primarily spatial, as objects and people are related through separation in and by space (Rapoport, 1977). The user preferences about using the built environment can be learnt through the study of man and built environment relationship. The focus for such a study has to be on man and his interface with the urban environment around, which is mostly built environment. Hence the spatial entity considered for the study is 'built environment'. The connecting mechanism of man with his surrounding (built) environment is a spatial experience. Consequently, the man and environment relationship can be comprehended by understanding the spatial experience. Spatial experience can be broken down to various parts:

1. Existing reality around, i.e. a built environment
2. Perception of the environment
3. Forming its images and schemata
4. Structuring of those images and schemata to form 'spatial cognition'
5. Use of the built environment for daily routine – spatial behaviour
6. Evaluation and evolution of built environment

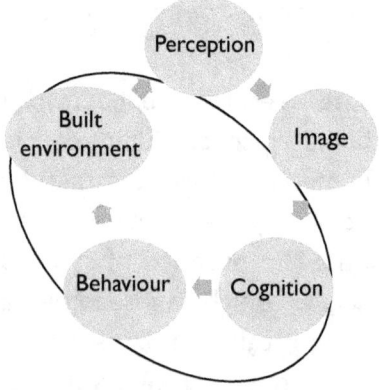

Figure 1.5 Spatial experience

All these components of 'spatial experience' (Fig. 1.5) form a continuum. The breakage is for understanding purpose. For the intended exploration, out of these components of the man–environment interface, built environment, its cognition and spatial behaviour are at focus.

1.3 Spatial cognition

The concept of natural movement is central to evolution of system of spaces in a built environment. It was believed till very recent past that spaces or spatial configuration in a built environment emerge due to functional requirements. Yet investigation till date has proved that spatial configurations are usually resultant of natural movement and not due to functional requirements (Hillier and Hanson, 1984). Thus, it is important to first understand that natural movement is a fundamental corelate of the way spatial configuration is shaped.

In an urban area, users move and use spaces on the basis of preferences and importance given, which can be termed as cognitive constructs. Cognitive constructs can be understood through study of user preferences. As a designer or planner, when one tries to deal with a built environment, this aspect of relationship between natural movement and user preferences, facilitated by configuration, is ignored.

Spatial configuration may facilitate or restrict the possibility for visual and physical linkages. While using the built environments, human beings try to structure the information about it to make it manageable. There is an evidence that man always made sense of the world through powerful simplifying abstractions which seek out the underlying principles and order in our experiences and perceptions (Batty and Longley, 1994). Cognition in anthropological sense is related to the making of places physical or social – by defining what is done, where and when, who is here or there and when, how here differs from there (Rapoport, 1977).

There is a subjective and an objective component of urban morphology. Spatial configuration as existing reality is the objective morphology, and the way people use it can be termed as subjective morphology. The spatial configuration is not directly responsible for the user behaviour. However, it is the subjective structuring of that configuration in terms of spatial cognition that is responsible for the behaviour. Thus spatial cognition is a mending mechanism between man and his environment (Rapoport, 1977). Planners/designers are continuously responsible for shaping spatial configurations through their interventions. Cognition is an important but subtle link and hence mostly overlooked. Cognition is context specific and varies from person to person. However, a society may have similar cognitive constructs. The author's position is not purely cognitive but 'socio-cognitive' (Gärdenfors, 2004), since constructs are not in the head of an individual. They are common for a group of the common language users with common cultural background.

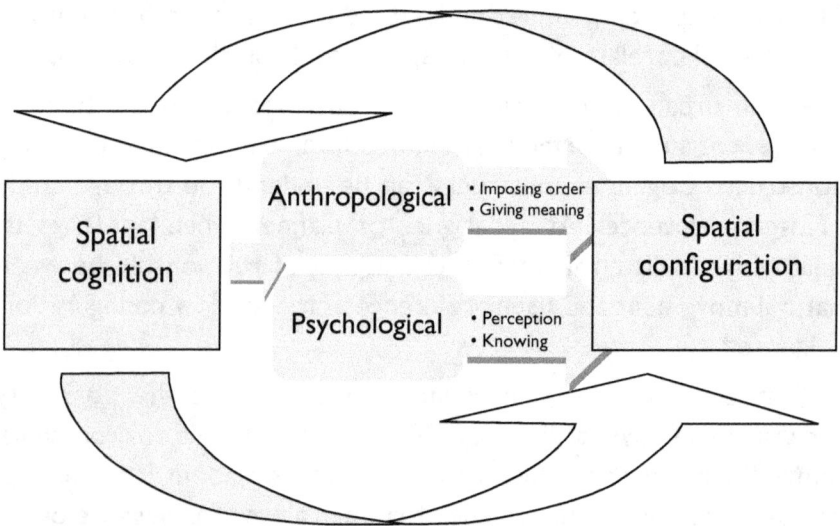

Figure 1.6 Relationship: Spatial configuration and spatial cognition

As shown in Fig. 1.6, the relationship between spatial cognition and configuration is two way. Spatial configuration is responsible for shaping cognition; and over the period of time, cognitive constructs shape spatial configuration. Spatial cognition has two views: one is related to psychological view and other is anthropological (Rapoport, 1977). Psychological view is about the correctness of schemata developed which depends on environmental knowledge. It varies with individual due to the variation in age, sex, experience, exposure to environment and spatial aptitude. However, the anthropological view is about process of imposing order on the existing built environment by the society. The cognitive constructs develop by attaching importance and meaning to the built environment. Psychological view and anthropological view are also related to each other. Built environments have discrete elements such as landmarks, paths, edges, nodes and districts. These are responsible for its imageability or visual qualities of the city. Imageability is associated with psychological aspect of cognition which is about 'knowing'. The anthropological aspect of built environment is about the relationship between these discrete elements of built environments which we may call as configuration. It is responsible for intelligibility of the built environment and the use of built environment. Thus we find ourselves needing, above all, an understanding of the city as a functioning physical and spatial object (Hillier, 1996). Hence, the anthropological view of cognition is required to be considered, as it tries to understand cognitive constructs as user preferences which are specific to a society due to common cultural background.

The study of relationship between spatial configuration and spatial cognition can help us to make explicit the cognitive constructs in terms of user preferences of a collective group. This understanding about man and built environment interface with its embedded cognitive constructs can help to evolve a methodological framework for cognitive approach while dealing urban environments in India.

1.4　Cognitive approach

In Indian developing cities, due to the pressing demand for land and built spaces, there is always a tussle between old and new. So the patterns of new spatial configurations are superimposed on old spatial configurations without actually understanding what is appropriate. The focus of the book is towards understanding and modelling topology of spaces on the basis of user preferences as cognitive constructs. Premise is that the study of relationship of spatial cognition and configuration will help to understand user preferences as principles of urbanism. This can then be used to evolve methodological framework for dealing built environment in context of Indian developing cities.

Exploration primarily tries to study:

(a) Commonalities of configuration in Indian context
(b) User preferences in traditional and contemporary built environments
(c) Effect on cognition due to spatial configuration and vice versa
(d) Modelling emerging built environments of urban India

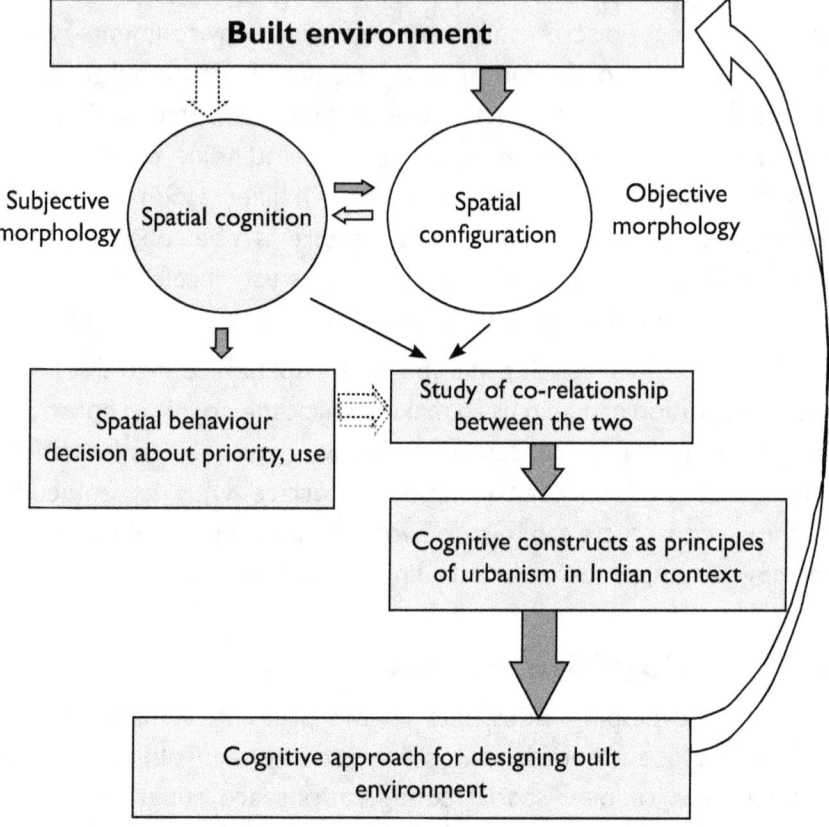

Figure 1.7 Investigation approach

As shown in Fig 1.7, built environment has spatial configuration (objective morphology). Spatial cognition of the users (subjective morphology) is reflected in the way users behave or use built environment. A concrete term for environment is a place (Schulz, 2003). Places do not make cities; it is cities that make places. The distinction is vital (Hillier, 1996). Hence, quality of individual place is not important but quality of relationships between places is important, if we are discussing spatial configuration and cognitive response. Relationships are important, and hence system of spaces needs to be represented and analysed as spatial configuration. For that, system of spaces needs to be considered with its topology rather than geometry of spaces. Topology and geometry are two different branches of mathematics which can describe objects/spaces in terms of their properties. Geometry describes specific, obvious form and shape. Topology helps to describe embedded structure and qualitative properties such as convergence, connectedness and continuity. Topologists study the large patterns and categories of shapes. The origins of topology date back to the 18th century; and the Konigsberg Bridge Problem – a problem of relative position without regard to distance was responsible for its emergence ('Topology,' 2012). Geometry can be the same yet topology may be different and vice versa. Spatial cognition is not a tangible entity and hence very difficult to externalize and comprehend. Spatial behaviour is an overt expression of spatial cognition (Markandey, 1997). Hence spatial behaviour in terms of the pattern of the use of spaces can help to understand cognitive constructs. On the basis of the study of the two, one can understand cognitive constructs as user preferences or principles of urbanism in Indian context. This can help us to evolve a cognitive approach for dealing built environments in urban India.

1.5 References

- Alexander, C. W. (1964). Notes on the Synthesis of Form. Cambridge, Massachusetts: Harvard University Press.
- Batty, M., and Longley, P. (1994). Fractal Cities: A Geometry of Form and Function (1st ed.). London: Academic Press.
- Clarke, Paul Walter (2003). The Economic Currency of Architectural Aesthetics. In Designing Cities: Critical Readings in Urban Design Edited by Cuthbert Alexander R. Oxford: Blackwell Publishers.
- Cuthbert, A. R. (Ed.) (2003). Designing Cities: Critical Readings in Urban Design (1st ed.). Oxford: Wiley-Blackwell.
- Desai, M. (2007). Traditional Architecture : House Form of the Islamic Community of Bohras in Gujarat. [New Delhi]: Council of Architecture.

- Gärdenfors, P. (2004). Conceptual Spaces: The Geometry of Thought. Cambridge: The MIT Press.
- Hillier, B. (1996). Space Is the Machine: A Configurational Theory of Architecture. Cambridge: Cambridge University Press. Electronic print Retrieved February 7, 2011 from eprints.ucl.ac.uk/3848/1/SpaceIsTheMachine_Part1.pdf
- Hillier, B., and Hanson, J. (1984). The Social Logic of Space. Cambridge: Cambridge University Press.
- Interview with Amos Rapoport (1992). In: Arch. & Comport. I Arch. & Behav, Vol. 8 (no. 1), pp. 93–102.
- Karimi, K. (1997). The Spatial Logic of Organic Cities in Iran and the United Kingdom. In Proceedings Volume I (Vol. I). Presented at the Space Syntax First International Symposium, London. Retrieved April 12, 2010 from http://www.spacesyntax.net/symposia-archive/SSS1
- Kostof, S. (1999). The City Shaped: Urban Patterns and Meanings Through History (Reprint). London: Thames & Hudson.
- Kumar, S. (1998). The Search for Spatial Order in Squatter Settlements: A Case Study of New Delhi, India. Montreal: McGill University.
- Lockton, D. (2011). Architecture, Urbanism, Design and Behaviour: a Brief Review. Design with Intent. Retrieved from http://architectures.danlockton.co.uk/2011/09/12/architecture-urbanism-design-and-behaviour-a-brief-review/
- Markandey, K. (1997). Spatial Cognition in Urban Development. Hyderabad, A.P.: University Publications and Press, Osmania University.
- McClure, W. R., and Bartuska, T. J. (Eds.). (2007). The Built Environment: A Collaborative Inquiry into Design and Planning (2nd ed.). Hoboken: John Wiley & Sons.
- Pandya, Y. (2004). Concept of Space: In Traditional Indian Architecture. Ahmedabad: Mapin Publishing Pvt. Ltd.
- Rapoport, A. (1969). House Form and Culture. Englewood Cliffs, New Jersey: Prentice-Hall.
- Rapoport, A. (1977). Human Aspects of Urban Form: Towards a Man-Environment Approach to Urban Form and Design (1st ed.). Oxford: Pergamon Press.
- Rapoport, A. (1979). On the Cultural Origins of Settlements. In A. J. Catanese and J. C. Synder (Eds.), Introduction to Urban Planning. New York: McGraw-Hill.
- Schulz, Christian Norberg. (2003). The Phenomena of Place. In Designing Cities: Critical Readings in Urban Design. Oxford: Blackwell Publishers.
- Topology. (2012, November 7). In Wikipedia, the Free Encyclopedia. Retrieved from http://en.wikipedia.org/w/index.php?title=Topology&oldid=521121542

Chapter 2

Photo: Framed view through a door of a village hut

Chapter 2

Urbanisation and urbanism in India

Abstract: This chapter talks about the urbanisation in India from past to present. India is in rapid phase of urbanization and has its contextual peculiarities in terms of its demographics and cultural diversity. Lack of proper understanding of urbanism in terms of user preferences is responsible for emergence of the chaotic spatial order in urban India, and it is becoming difficult to deal the problems of rapid urbanization. This necessitates the development of new vision for urban planning practices in India.

Key words: Urbanisation, urbanism, user preferences, planning practices, plan process

2.1 Urbanisation and urbanism

India is emerging as one of the populous countries. It is gaining importance in world scenario not only due to its population, but also due to pace of economic development. It has its own contextual peculiarities in terms of its urbanization, demographics and cultural diversity. As per the 2011 census of India, its population is 1.21 billion people and it has emerged second most populated country in the world ('Census of India 2011,' n.d.). It is not just the population size, but the population has vast magnitude of variations in terms of ethnic groups, religions, languages and castes. The population is distributed in considerably varying climatic regions. Further, complexity is added by the variation that occurs across this population on socio-economic parameters such as income and education. No other country except the continent of Africa exceeds the linguistic, genetic and cultural diversity that exists in India. Twenty first century is mostly being referred as 'urban century' of 'global south' (Roy, 2011). India is a developing country and the urbanization process is still continuing. The trend of urbanization in India is very much characteristic as compared to other developing countries. Initially, the percentage increase in urban population was less compared to the increase in total population. Thus urbanization in India has been relatively slow compared to many developing countries; but at present, India is in the accelerated stage of urbanization (Dutta, 2006). Urbanism in India is as peculiar as the urbanization. All the diverse and peculiar aspects of urbanization are responsible for equally peculiar urbanism in India.

Cities are characterized as 'urban' by their size, density and heterogeneity. Urbanism is about the way of life that gets emerged in cities. Wikipedia ('Urbanism,' 2012) defines urbanism as the study of how inhabitants of towns and cities interact with the built environment. Urbanism has many facets quoted by Kostof (1993) such as:

- *Religion* – physical organization displays a deliberate program of ritual intent
- *Politics and governance* – ease of governance and security concerns

- *Primacy of ruler and his military shield*
- *Display of power through vista and axiality*
- *Social order* – intensions of interactions and control

Thus urbanism focuses on the geography, economy, politics and social characteristics of the urban environment, as well as the effects on and caused by the built environment. Facets of urbanism such as religion, security concerns, primacy of ruler and display of power through vista and axiality have almost lost their relevance. Yet the facets of urbanism such as social order, control and ease of governance still have a lot of implications on contemporary built environments. By urbanism, the author means as cognitive constructs of users for social behaviour. These constructs and preferences of users significantly affect the built environments. As planner/designer, one needs to be aware of constructs and principles of urbanism, so as to avoid conflicts between the way designer designs and the way users prefer.

2.2   Contemporary planning practices

History of India and its civilization dates back to at least 6500 BC, which is one of the oldest surviving civilizations in the world. It has a long history of settlement planning since Indus valley civilization with cities like Mohenjo Daro and Harappa. Throughout its history, many invaders have come to India but Indian religions allowed it to adapt and absorb all of them. India has always been simply too big, too complicated, and too culturally subtle to let an empire dominate it for long. Based on archeological findings, Indian history can be broadly divided into five phases ('Indian History,' n.d.):

1. Saraswati (Harappan) civilization: 6500 BC to 1000 BC or also called 'Vedic period' in history of India.
2. Golden period of Indian History: 500 BC to 800 AD
3. Muslim influence in India: 1000 AD to 1700 AD
4. British period in India: 1700 AD to 1947 AD
5. Modern India: 1947 to till date

Various theories, movements and people have shaped the urbanisation and the cities in India. The new value system based on urban planning principles was accepted in post-industrial revolution period. These can be traced back to the year 1898 when the Bombay Improvement Act came into force. Under the Act, there was institution of Bombay Improvement Trust (BIT), which was empowered to draft and implement town planning schemes in the area of its jurisdiction. This was in accordance with the political intentions of British then and was significant from planning point of view. This indicated awareness toward subjecting physical growth of urban areas to planning schemes. Planning meant then as certain minimum width of roads and satisfaction of certain subdivision regulations. After that, similar improvement trusts were established in other cities such as Agra, Kanpur, Nagpur, Delhi and Kolkata, which still exist. Municipalities were then under Indian governance and were responsible for maintaining facilities and services.

Another important milestone event in the development of Indian urban planning practices was the visit of Patrick Geddes in 1920. He was invited to India to advice some conceptual framework within which planning activity should be performed. Geddes introduced the concept of conservative surgery and diagnosis before treatment (Tyrwhitt, 1947). He also introduced the concept of comprehensive surveys and emphasized that planning is not to be interpreted in limited 'physical sense'. Rather, it is multidisciplinary in nature, covering the socioeconomic aspects of cities. Thus, he introduced ideological base for planners and administrators in India.

In post-independence period, the major influence was through the new cities such as Chandigarh, designed by Le Corbusier. The town planning acts that were developed in each state guided the urban planning practices in post-independence period till date. Like most of the colonized countries, India also follows the planning legacy based on the principles of segregation which was followed in British or European planning legislations. Land management, land-use planning and zoning are the primary planning premises of all these acts. These land management mechanisms through master planning play an important role in spatial order that is emerging in urban

India. The more flexible mechanisms of structure and strategic plans have evolved but it's also based on the underlying concept of land management and zoning. Thus, in India, most of the issues related to built environment are still dealt with rational approach of urban planning.

2.3 User preferences

The general plan process for dealing urban environments can be summarized as shown in Fig. 2.1.

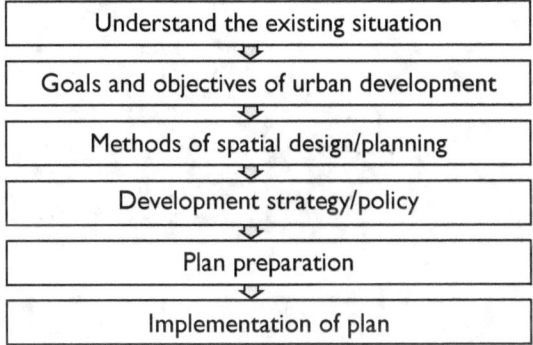

Figure 2.1 Plan process

In India, the planners, architects and designers are mostly responsible for policies, standards and actions in terms of master plans and building plans. The decisions about planning objectives and goals are taken by bureaucrats and politicians. The user preferences are either ignored or the rationalistic values are authoritatively imposed. There is a strong relationship between values and urban form. Rapoport (1977) has also emphasised on the same fact that general public and planners/designers at times represent different value systems, and values of users/non-designers or general public are rarely considered. Because of lack of proper method to understand user preferences, the kind of spatial order that is emerging in urban India, it is becoming difficult to deal the problems of rapid urbanization. Spatial order based on the paradigm of rationality and orderliness has been grossly adopted. This necessitates the development of new vision for urban planning practices in India. There are other

Figure 2.2 Temple, hawkers on the street ...order imposed by users

mechanisms to understand the preferences of a society under consideration such as public participatory planning. Participatory planning paradigm is quite relevant but in country like India with its diversities and lack of education, it may not give comprehensive picture about user preferences. There are issues related to their technical know-how, influences and non-realization of subconscious needs which they are not themselves aware of. User preferences if not taken care of appropriately in plan process, we would find emergence of conflicting situations due to a tussle between spatial configuration and the way people use it (social order). The process of imposing order by users is often experienced in Indian cities.

Commercial, religious, social activities and community gathering spaces emerge in urban areas, especially along streets due to this process of imposing order. Figure 2.2 shows a conflicting situation in urban areas wherein a temple is built on the street turning or hawkers sell goods on heavy traffic streets. Hence, there is a need to evolve a methodological framework, by which human preferences can be understood and taken care of properly while framing the goals. It can contribute in making the plan process for dealing the urban environments much more context specific and help in making built environments much more humane. The study of relationship of spatial configuration and spatial cognition can help us to decipher cognitive constructs as user preferences. This can initiate innovative and relevant methods of spatial design as against the current planning practices adopted to deal contemporary built environments in urban India.

2.4 References

- Census of India: Provisional Population Totals India: Paper I: Census 2011. (n.d.). Retrieved September 9, 2011, from http://www.censusindia.gov.in/2011-prov-results/prov_results_paper1_india.html
- Dutta, P. (2006). *Urbanisation in India* (pp. 2–16). Presented at the Regional and Sub-Regional Population Dynamic Population Process in Urban Areas. European Population Conference. Retrieved February 26, 2010 from http://www.infostat.sk/vdc/epc2006/papers/epc2006s60134.pdf
- Indian History. (n.d.). Retrieved September 17, 2012, from http://www.gatewayforindia.com/history.htm

- Kostof, S. (1999). *The City Shaped: Urban Patterns and Meanings Through History* (Reprint). London: Thames & Hudson.
- Rapoport, A. (1977). *Human Aspects of Urban Form: Towards a Man-Environment Approach to Urban Form and Design* (1st ed.). Oxford: Pergamon Press.
- Roy, A. (2011). Lecture, University of California, Berkeley.
- Tyrwhitt, J. (1947). *Patrick Geddes in India*. Lund Humphries.
- Wikipedia contributors (2012a). Urbanism. In Wikipedia, the Free Encyclopedia. Wikimedia Foundation, Inc. Retrieved from http://en.wikipedia.org/w/index.php?title=Urbanism&oldid=510814548

Chapter 3

Photo: Galli Cricket, Lane in Mominpura, Nagpur

Chapter 3

Spatial configuration and cognition

Abstract: In this chapter, the synthesis of various theories related to a built environment, are studied to create a framework to investigate the relationship between spatial configuration and spatial cognition. It has formulated the required epistemological basis for the intended investigation about user preferences and principles of Indian urbanism. Thus, the study of number of identified theories related to urban design, urban morphology, morphogenesis, social and spatial order, urban structure, spatial design and spatial modelling is done to formulate pragmatic approach for comprehending user preferences.

Key words: Space syntax, space proxemics, concept of depth, cognitive mapping, spatial design

3.1 Epistemological basis

Various theorists such as Lewis Mumford, Jane Jacobs, Amos Rapoport, Kevin Lynch, Christopher Alexander, Hillier and Hanson and their theories about socio spatial aspects of built environment are referred.

3.1.1 Lewis Mumford

Lewis Mumford (1961) was one of the pioneers whose thinking about urban affairs was not limited up to narrow matters of physical planning; he talked about social implications as well. For Mumford, Sir Patrick Geddes' work provided the basic direction and the skeleton to which he then added. Mumford was also deeply interested in India. He studied Indian history and religion and closely followed Geddes' town planning work in India ('City Renewal: Lewis Mumford,' n.d.).

The city was then purely considered as a physical fact. Lewis Mumford raised the question about 'city as a social institution' (Mumford, 1961) and talked about social aspects of a city in 'The Culture of the Cities'. He mentioned that 'the city is the form and symbol of an integrated social relationship' and 'point of maximum concentration for the power and culture of a community' (Kostof, 1999, p.37). The nature of the city is not to be found simply in its economic base. The city is primarily a social emergent. He always criticized the structure of modern cities. These primarily result out of technological advancement of human race and changed economic policies such as capitalism. He argued that the structure of modern cities is responsible for many social problems and emphasized organic relationship between people and their living spaces. Modern cities lack the clarity about the social notion of the city. The earlier planners and their town planning efforts did not anticipate that merely building sanitary tenements or widening narrow streets will not suffice this notion of the city.

'The physical design of cities and their economic functions are secondary to their relationship to the natural environment and to the spiritual values of human community' (Wikipedia contributors, 2012c). Though contemporary planning practices in India are based on Geddes' philosophy, still there is a need to investigate city as a social institution and further the humane approach advocated by Mumford in Indian context.

3.1.2 Jane Jacobs

When the man and built environment relationship in urban context is at focus, the most important living space is the urban neighbourhood. Jane Jacobs through her seminal work of 'The Death and Life of Great American Cities' (Jacobs, 1992) emphasized the importance of neighbourhoods. The book is a critique of modernist planning policies. Jacobs claimed that these policies were destroying many existing inner-city communities. She strongly criticized 'rationalist American planners' like Robert Moses. She argued that modernist city planning practices reject city and more importantly reject human beings living in communities that are characterized by complexity and chaos. The generalized and deductive kind or reasoning used for planning usually advocated separation of uses. These planning practices, she claimed, destroy neighbourhoods and innovative economies by creating universal, isolated and unnatural urban spaces. The four generators of diversity advocated by her are mixed uses activating streets at different times of the day, short blocks allowing high pedestrian permeability, buildings of various ages and states of repair and last is density. Her aesthetic sense was then considered opposite to that of the modernists, upholding redundancy and vibrancy, against order and efficiency (Wikipedia contributors, 2012d).

Jane Jacobs mainly focused on the local neighbourhoods of New York, which were getting destroyed due to major urban renewal projects to accommodate transportation requirements of automobile age. Yet her arguments have been identified as universal. They certainly hold true for medium-size developing cities in India where the traditional built environments or living, vibrant neighbourhoods are getting affected. Also, the emerging built environments are as per the modern planning practices, neglecting the user preferences.

3.1.3 Amos Rapoport

Amos Rapoport continued the emphasis on man–environment relationship and its importance for design and planning of built environment. Being an anthropologist and architect himself, he had highlighted a need to develop the scientific approach to the built environment through environment behaviour investigation. He termed the stream of designing the physical setting as environmental design and the study of relationship of man with his physical environment as environment behaviour studies (Rapoport, 1977, p.1).

Man–environment relationship is primarily spatial. The spatial configuration of the environment is, therefore, the result of the application of sets of rules which reflect differing concepts of environmental quality. The set of values or rules of spatial organization are different for different groups (Rapoport, 1977, p.24). The socio-cultural factors such as life values and priorities (what you give importance to) keep on changing with time, place and people. Hence, the first and emergent need is to understand the built-in values and rules of a given spatial configuration. These values and rules will certainly affect the definition of problems, the data used and solutions produced, while dealing built environments through spatial design (Rapoport, 1977, p.24). It was generally thought that climate, available building material, local topography were the most influential factors shaping built environments. Instrumental in challenging this deterministic and non-cultural view, Rapoport demonstrated that people were not passive slaves to their environment. Instead they used culture and architecture to modify their physical environment rather than the other way round (Moore and Duffy, 2000, p.9).

Discussing the importance and role of human response in shaping built environment, he has mentioned that human response shapes the environment, and subsequently environmental perception and cognition is responsible for user behaviour. The question of what effect the physical environment has on people has received attention in cultural geography and in environmental design investigation (Rapoport, 1977, p.2). According to him, there seem to have been three attitudes in geography.

1. *Environmental determinism* – The view that the physical environment determines the human behaviour.
2. *Possibilism* – The view that the physical environment provides possibilities and constraints within which people make choices based on other, mainly cultural criteria.
3. *Probabilism* – The current view that the physical environment does, in fact, provide possibilities for choice and is not determining, but that some choices are more probable than others in physical settings.

Thus the view of probabilism is considered for the investigation is that built environment can be seen as setting for human activities. Physical settings may be inhibiting or facilitating certain kind of behaviour; though it will not totally dictate the behaviour.

Amos Rapoport has also argued that the environmental effects are mediated by the 'filters' in the mind. The perceived environment is structured on the basis of culture-specific meanings. This process of structuring environmental information is called cognition. Cognition, from the Latin word for 'getting to know', basically describes the way people give meaning to the physical world which affects design and behaviour (Rapoport, 1977, p.109). Cognition is then a search for order and a process of imposing an order – the type of order varying with the cognitive style of particular groups. Users always tend to impose certain spatial and social order through processes of perception, orientation and behaviour. Thus, the basic cognitive act is the placing of the individual in his physical and social milieu (Rapoport, 1977, p.109). The cognition for users get developed over a period of time and spatial behaviour is closely related to cognitive map than physical map of built environment (Fig. 3.1).

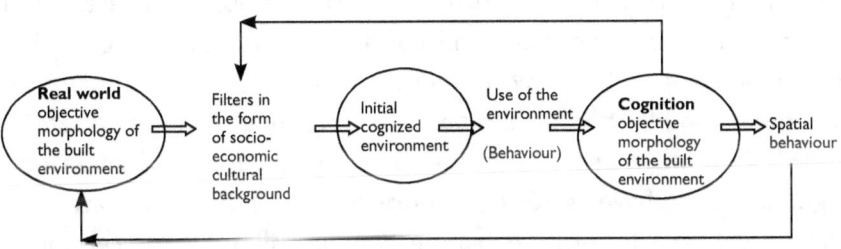

Figure 3.1 Development of spatial cognition

It is very unlikely that people have cognitive schemata for megalopolis, but cognitive definition extends significantly to immediate surroundings such as neighbourhood. When we consider an area with some homogeneity and contiguity, it is usually termed as neighbourhood. The neighbourhoods have varied definitions and also have differential importance for different groups and populations depending on culture, context, the social system, etc. Yet, the simple and common characteristic of a neighbourhood is that it is an area intermediate between the dwelling and the whole city, which is better known, with which one has more identification (however minimal) than the larger, unknown area. It becomes a figure against the ground of the city (Rapoport Amos, 1980). Thus, though it is physical entity, basically it is a cognitive construct. Certainly, the physical aspects of the built environment in terms of spatial configuration will affect the cognitive constructs of a neighbourhood. Neighbourhood leads to formation of 'sense of belonging' and definition of 'my own area'. In case of small and medium cities in India, as they are developing, the concept and role of neighbourhood as immediate living space or link between home and city is getting disturbed. It is having a lot of implications on social environment in these cities.

This does not mean that these growing cities should not develop, but there is a need to understand the user preferences in terms of the cognitive constructs about their immediate surroundings, i.e. neighbourhoods. This will help to maintain the coherent harmonious link between a house, a neighbourhood and a city.

3.1.4   Kevin Lynch

Kevin Lynch is one of the pioneer urban planners who contributed profoundly to the field of city planning through empirical investigation on how individuals perceive and navigate the urban landscape. He described 'image of an environment' through its identity, structure and meaning. His books explore how urban environments affect users. Also how users organize the physical form of cities and regions so as to have better perception and use. It has formulated the conceptual basis for good urban design and still holds the relevance in contemporary times. Lynch's most famous work *The Image of the*

City (Lynch, 1992), first published in 1960, is the result of a 5-year study on how users perceive and organize spatial information as they navigate through cities. Using three distinct cities Boston, Jersey City, and Los Angeles as examples, Lynch reported that users understood their surroundings in consistent and predictable ways, forming mental maps with five elements:

- *Paths:* Paths are the streets, sidewalks, trail, transit lines, canals, railroads and other channels in which people travel. They are the channels along which the observer customarily, occasionally, or potentially moves.
- *Edges:* These are perceived boundaries such as buildings, shorelines, railroad cut, edges of development and walls. Edges are linear elements not used or considered as paths by observers. They are the boundaries between two phases and are linear breaks in physical and visual continuity.
- *Districts:* These are relatively large sections of the city distinguished by some identity or character due to homogeneity. Districts are medium-sized subsections of the city that one may enter and feel 'inside of', such as a business center, campus, or residential neighbourhood.
- *Nodes:* Nodes are points or the strategic spots in a city into which an observer can enter, and are the foci of intensive activities to and from which he/she travels. They may be primarily junctions, places of a break in transportation, a crossing or convergence of paths, or moments of shift from one structure to another. In India, nodes are usually characterized by congregation of number of users for some activity.
- *Landmarks:* These are readily identifiable objects which serve as external reference points. Landmarks are external points of references for the observers. Landmarks usually possess some distinctive form that contrasts with background information. Examples are tall buildings, buildings with distinctive colors or large bulk, and distinctive structures.

He focused on the role of these discrete elements of physical environments for orientation of the user in the space. He is the person who coined some of the important terms such as 'imageability', 'identity', 'wayfinding' and 'legibility'.

Furthering the work about urban environment and human aspects of it, Kevin Lynch in his another influential work *Good City Form* (Lynch, 1998) has listed the performance dimensions of a good urban environment. The identified performance dimensions are mentioned below:

- *Vitality* – Ability to support biological functioning of life through sustenance, safety and consonance
- *Sense* – The clarity with which the environment can be perceived and identified, linked and rendered meaningful through identity, structure, congruence, transparency, legibility and significance
- *Fit* – The match between behaviour of people and the spatial pattern of their settlements through adequacy and adaptability
- *Access* – The extent to which people are connected with other people, places, goods, activities and information
- *Control* – The extent to which the users of a place regulate it

Apart from these, he also listed two meta-criteria such as efficiency and justice.

The investigation focuses on relationship of man and his physical environment. Out of the five elements of imageability, paths, nodes and landmarks are identified as relevant. The performance indicators, sense and fit are relevant. Psychological aspect of cognition is related to imageability of the environment. It will come under the performance dimension 'sense' wherein discrete elements such as landmarks, nodes and districts will play a role. Anthropological aspect of cognition is related to performance dimension 'fit' as it talks about user preferences as against the designed environment. Based on the understanding developed through the study of Lynch's theory, methodological framework is developed.

3.1.5 Christopher Alexander

In the book, *A Pattern Language: Towns, Buildings, Construction* (Alexander, Ishikawa and Silverstein, 1977), Christopher Alexander described a practical architectural system that a theoretical mathematician or computer scientist might call a generative grammar (Wikipedia contributors, 2012e).

In the successive work titled *Timeless Way of Building*, Christopher Alexander (1979) described the coherence between the building design and its use. Such coherence always existed in historic buildings but somehow lost in modern times. Christopher Alexander produced some profound theories about generative grammar of built environments, may it be a building or a city. Users know more about the buildings they need than any architect could. The generative rules as grammar, if understood, the designer's role can be to apply it appropriately in given place, time and for given users. This understanding about planning and design is quite profound, and there is a need to develop such an understanding peculiarly about Indian built environments from users' perspective.

In the book *A New Theory of Urban Design'* (Christopher, 1987), he advocated alternative to master planning and also gave understanding about the generative process of evolution of towns and cities which seem to be shanty or chaotic to planners and designers.

In the most recent works by him in the form of four volumes of *The Nature of Order* (Alexander Christopher, 2004), he has tried to construct a coherent picture of life on earth. According to him, till date, most of the theories had a divide between fact and value. Facts get explained, evaluated and improved with science yet values that are so important in everyday life are not addressed by philosophy of science.

Everything on earth, may it be natural or manmade, has a structure in terms of hierarchies and interconnectivities. In nature, though the structure is changing or rather evolving, the wholeness and harmony are continued. According to him, when we look at architecture of modern cities, it is certainly obvious that human beings can manage and make terrible mess of their surroundings. He compared the transformations in nature to transformations in built environment. Changes/transformations are inevitable. In nature, transformations are characterized by special kind of harmony, beauty and wholeness, and it comes without any effort. These he termed as structure preserving or wholeness transforming transformations. According to him, in urban areas, there is wholeness disrupting transformations.

He has made an interesting observation that in spite of endless variety of configurations found in nature, one can distil them down to 15 geometric properties or classes of organization to be understood as the generative codes for them and then apply that knowledge to urban environs (Alexander, 2004, p.144). He has also stated that the formation of a single object or in the piecemeal aggregation of town requires the sort of generative process, a careful deliberate sequence of steps in which each step creates the context for the next one and each next wholeness is determined from the previous wholeness (Alexander, 2002, p.23). Christopher Alexander has presented an idea that a living process always has enormous respect for the state and the morphology of what exists and always finds the next step forward. It preserves the structure of what exists, develops and extends its latent structure (Alexander, 2003, p.23). Hence, as a designer or planner of the built environment, first of all we need to understand the existing structure and its generative rules.

As stated by Alexander (2004), 'Our role as creator of built environment is to create life in the fabric of space itself '. Thus, he has explained the concept of 'life' in anything around us, including built environment as the one which has 'order'. 'Order' is resultant of complex patterns generated by interacting rules and a computable generative process (Alexander, 2004, p.9). The 'built environments' can be termed as 'living' if they are not only 'changing' but 'evolving' (Alexander, 2003, p.131). Thus, if changes for future are based on present, it can be termed as evolution. To deal built environments in future, one should deduce the configuration of existing built environments in terms of their hierarchies and interconnectivities. On the basis of that understanding, we can evolve built environments for future use.

3.1.6 Hillier and Hanson

Bill Hillier and Julienne Hanson in their work *Social Logic of Space* (Hillier and Hanson, 1984) brought forward the fact that though we prefer to discuss architecture and built environment in terms of visual styles, its put hyphen practical effects are not at the level of appearances at all, but are at the level of space. Spatial configuration in a built environment acts as preconditions for patterns of movement, encounter and avoidance which are the generators of social life. The book outlined a new theory and method for the investigation of user–space relationship. Though quite similar to Christopher Alexander's work based on notion of syntactic generators (Hillier and Hanson, 1984, p.11), the theory essentially gives more quantifiable and tangible approach for understanding spatial configuration in terms of hierarchies and interconnectedness. Spatial configuration is a set of relationship between parts and the whole which can define spatial structure (Hillier, 1996, p.24).

For analyzing configuration, it is important to understand built environment as a system of spaces. Configuration plays a prime role of physical and visual linkages. The metric distance between the spaces is influential than the depth distance. The topology of spaces is more important than the geometry of spaces. They have also defined structure and order. Spatial systems are intelligible to us in two ways: as artefacts, we move about and learn to understand by living in (Hillier, 1996, p.186). Thus, spatial structure is the objective morphology of spaces in a built environment, and social order is subjective morphology which is developed by living in. Social order may be thought of as the outcome of social and physiological processes through which individuals form bonds and become linked into social system. In this sense, social order is as meant by Amos Rapoport as spatial cognition in anthropological view. According to Rapoport, cognition in anthropological view is about imposing order.

Thus, Hillier and Hanson stated that there is a strong link between spatial configuration and social implications, which needs to be identified and studied using theory and method of space syntax.

3.2　Comprehension of user preferences

The diverse and peculiar aspects of urbanization are responsible for equally peculiar urbanism in India. In the investigation, by urbanism the author means as cognitive constructs of users for social behaviour. These constructs and preferences of users significantly affect the built environments. As planners and designers, one needs to be aware of constructs and principles of urbanism, so as to avoid conflicts between the way designer designs and the way users prefer. Urban planning practices in India are based on British post-industrial revolution planning theories and policies. As the user preferences substantially vary from planned physical environment, it leads to number of conflicts. Such conflicting situations are termed as illegal, informal, etc. Hence, there is a need to understand user preferences and frame principles of urbanism in Indian context. For that, there is a need of studying man–environment relationship, and cognition is the important link.

Lewis Mumford was one of the pioneer philosophers and planners who emphasized social implication of planning. Jane Jacobs through her work for neighbourhoods in New York highlighted the implications of modern planning practices based on mechanistic and rational approach on communities and its physical settings. She also highlighted that mixing uses, vibrancy and chaos is essential in urban setting so as to make it humane. It certainly holds true in Indian context. Amos Rapoport coined the term environment behaviour studies to highlight the man–environment relationship. He also mentioned a mending mechanism between man and environment as environmental cognition. He has stated three attitudes for study of cultural geography. Out of which, not the concept of physical determinism but the concept of environmental probabilism, where the role of environment is to offer possibilities and choices, forms the base of the investigation. The settings may be inhibiting or facilitating certain kind of behaviour though it will not totally dictate the behaviour.

Kevin Lynch initiated empirical investigation on perception and cognition of urban environment. Cognition has discrete and relational properties. The five elements – paths, nodes, districts, edges and landmarks – are discrete elements of cognition.

Christopher Alexander talked about structure and order. Everything has structure including built environment in terms of configuration. It can be understood as hierarchies and interconnectivities. According to him, it needs to be understood as generative codes in order to deal with them appropriately, so that the transformations are not structure disturbing. There are few other important urban theorists who dealt design and analysis of urban built environment. Edmund C. Bacon's *Design of Cities* (1974) though talked about axial relationships between spaces which influenced visual fields and movement within spaces; however, it did not give analytical framework to understand possible generative processes. Many other urban theorists have also given analytical models for study of urban spaces such as Rob Krier. Most of them including Krier's theory of urban space (Krier, 1979) focuses on urban morphology w.r.t geometry and not topology. Batty and Longley (1994) tried to apply fractal geometries to cities in terms of their shapes and morphology. No doubt these theories are quite helpful in understanding cities in terms of their geometry, morphology and simulation, modelling. Yet, the theories do not refer to topology of spaces and social content of the spatial system and hence not considered for the intended investigation. Hillier and Hanson through their seminal work, 'Social Logic of Space' gave a possible analytical framework and tool which could describe topology of spaces. The analytical tool helps to understand not only generative processes of urban built environments but also the implication of spatial structure on social order. Through the book, they outline a theory and method to investigate spatial configuration. It is the identified theoretical premise for the investigation.

3.3 Spatial configuration

Spatial configuration is defined as a relation affected by the simultaneous co-presence of at least a third element and possibly all other elements in a complex (Hillier, 1996, p.71). 'We easily recognize configurations without conscious thought and just as easily use configurations in everyday life without thinking of them; but we do not know what it is we recognize and we are not conscious of what it is we use and how we use it' (Hillier, 1996, p.28). Thus, spatial configuration or structure is a set of relations between spaces that exists at a particular point in time.

There are various methods of analyzing built environment. Most of them depend on visual and physical aspects, metric distances and geometrical aspects of configuration. Usually, built environment is understood by its architectural style and its relation to socio-political and economic events. The main emphasis of such approaches is to analyze the architectural style and characters, activities within the urban fabric, and to examine the other issues related to the environmental and physical conditions of buildings. However, such methods apparently lack in perceiving the 'spatial configuration and social behaviour relationship' (Nabil, 2009). As already discussed, analysis till date suggests that far-reaching practical implications on human response are not because of visual appearance but of spatial configuration. Quality of individual space is not important but quality of relationship between spaces is important, if we are discussing spatial configuration and user response. Relationships are important, and hence spatial configuration needs to be represented and analyzed as a system of spaces. System of spaces needs to be considered with its topology rather than geometry of spaces. Space syntax is one method to understand the topological relationships of a space to all other spaces. The notion of syntax, derived from linguistics, refers to relationships between different spaces, or interactions between space and society (Bin and Christophe, 2002).

As already discussed, Hillier and Hanson (1984) for the first time presented the theoretical ideas for quantifying spatial configuration on the basis of topological distance. The theory and methods given by them are termed as Space Syntax. They suggest that in both cities and buildings, the relationship between form, its function and users is primarily spatial. The fundamental correlate of the spatial configuration is movement (Hillier, 1996, p.113). Movement largely dictates the configuration of spaces in the city, and movement is largely determined by spatial configuration. Based on empirical studies, Hillier (1996, p.113) argues that 'the structure of the urban grid, considered purely as a spatial configuration, is itself the most powerful single determinant of urban movement, both pedestrian and vehicular. It has already been a powerful force in shaping our historically evolved cities by its effect on land-use patterns, building densities, the mixing of uses in urban area and the part to whole relationship or structure of a city' (Hillier, 1996, p.152). The overall distribution of movement and subsequently the social order and cohesion in the area are largely determined by spatial configuration. Space syntax methodology is all about understanding system of spaces in terms of its configuration properties and hence selected as major theoretical premise for the investigation undertaken. Thus, with the help of space syntax methodology, one can develop an approach to study the way social and spatial aspects simultaneously affect each other at both micro and macro level, in Indian built environments.

3.4   Configuration: Socio-cultural implications

Built environments can be defined as organization of space w.r.t. time and are made up of fixed, semi-fixed, non-fixed features (Rapoport, 1982, p.87). All these features and human beings exist in 'a space'. 'Space' as a concept can be studied in variety of contexts. The Oxford English Dictionary gives the meaning as 'a continuous expanse in which things exist and move'. The physical attribute of space is a form which means shape, configuration, structure, pattern, organization, system of relations. The science of form is morphology (Oxford University Press, 2007). Urban morphology may, then, be categorized as the systematic study of the form, shape, plan, structure and functions of the built fabric of towns and cities, and of the origin and the way in which built environment has evolved over time (Madani-Pour, 1996).

As mentioned earlier, collectively the products and processes of human creation are called the built environment. Bartuska (McClure et al., 2007) has defined the built environment by four interrelated characteristics:

- First, it is extensive, is everywhere, provides the context for all human endeavors and everything humanly created, modified, arranged and maintained.
- It is intended to serve human needs, wants and values and hence result of human purpose.
- It is created to help us to deal with, protect us to mediate or change this environment for our comfort and well-being.

- Every component of the built environment is shaped by context. Each of the individual elements contributes either positively or negatively to the overall quality of environment, either built or natural, and to man–environment relationship.

Various issues related to built environment are environmental, technological and socio-cultural.

Social and cultural issues deal with why people build. This points to the fact that settlements across the globe vary notably in physical configurations but also in the 'degree to which ordering of space appears as a conspicuous dimension of culture.' It could be that different types of society requires different kinds of control on encounters in order to the type of society (Hillier and Hanson, 1984, p.4). Environmental issues deal with the natural and built context, locally and globally. And finally, technological issues deal with the materials, energy and financial resources, methods, and systems required to establish interrelationships and construct the built environment. All issues are interrelated and equally important. The focus for the investigation is on social cultural issues. These are important issues as they tell us why we build, how and why the way we build.

Culture presents a code for abstracting and symbolizing behaviour. Human response to the environment is mediated by symbols, which are, in turn, determined by cultural attitudes and values (Kumar, 1998). Culture depicts the 'way of life' for a community. It consists of habits, ways of thinking and thoughts and norms for social behaviour. The spatial configuration of any environment is dictated by the socio-economic levels and cultural values of the people using the space. Thus, the varieties of culture prevalent in different societies, therefore, contribute to the diversity of spatial forms. These cultural variations through time and across the globe today highlight that the human interaction with the environment is active rather than passive and hence human response to space is variable (Kumar, 1998).

Human needs get manifested in built environment at various levels. Physical and physiological needs are related to individual building level. Social needs are catered by built environments at city level. Psychological needs get manifested in non-physical aspects of built environment such as culture, identity and sense of place (McClure et al., 2007). Thus, sociocultural values are another important determinant of built environment. This viewpoint is further elaborated by Rapoport (1979), 'the way cities, regions and countries look depend, in the final analysis on the design activity of many individuals and groups at different times' (pp. 35). Values may be more abstract than needs, but a general understanding of them can enhance our sensitivity to the attitudes people have about the built environment. Value-formed attitudes manifest themselves in the way we relate to our surroundings, and the way we solve problems. Thus, values affect subjective attitudes, and many of these find expression in the built environment. For example, many Americans place a high value on individual rights and freedoms. It is reflected in the built environments that are created there. Formality associated with every activity is reflected in the formal nature of built environment. Instead, Indian society is very much based on the values of interdependency, interpersonal relationships and personal attachments, interference, involvement. Hence, there is lot of informal character to many activities and spaces required for them. It is difficult to make explicit such subjective values, attitudes and their role in shaping built environments. Since, design and planning can be defined as the art and science of creatively resolving issues, and of solving inherent conflicts in man–environmental relationships, we as planners/designers need to understand such subjective attitudes and values.

Thus, there are certainly some peculiarities of socio-cultural issues in Indian context, which are responsible for shaping the kind of built environments in India, throughout the history. For dealing these multilayered built environments in contemporary time, it is necessary to understand peculiarities and reasons. The point is not to find out which values are better, as science is always ethically neutral. The point is to evolve a methodological approach where we can try to understand and decode values of a given society from its built environment, before we go further in dealing them. Spatial cognition is an approach, and the study of relationship of spatial configuration and spatial cognition can help us to understand values as user preferences.

3.4.1 Social cohesion

Human beings establish relationship with built environment through use and movement. Though space may be physical entity, it can be defined as social space. It has tremendous social implications in terms of providing possibilities, choices for physical and visual linkages. It is through the society's realization in space that we can recognize its very existence. A society not only does exist in space but also is defined by locating people in space to give rise to varying patterns of movement and encounter (Hillier and Hanson, 1984, pp. 26–27). The social order or the way social relationship and interactions get shaped in a built environment is a physiological, psychological and social phenomenon (Barchas and Mendoza, 1984). The social phenomenon about social interaction and behaviour is termed as social cohesion.

Social cohesion is a term used in social policy, sociology and political science to describe the bonds or 'glue' that bring people together in society, particularly in the context of cultural diversity (Wikipedia contributors, 2012e). Social cohesion is a multi-faceted notion covering many different kinds of social phenomena. The meaning of this concept can differ according to socio-political environment. For Indian context, social cohesion is not about homogeneity but about sharing some common values to achieve social integration or social inclusion. There are inequalities in Indian society. The objective of all planning and development issues is to cope with inequalities and disparities. Disparities are going to be there in societies but a cohesive society is one which has developed satisfactory ways of coping with these in a open and democratic manner (Jenson & Commonwealth Secretariat, 2010). For social cohesion, social encounters are necessary. Built environment through its possibility of restricting or establishing visual and physical linkages is responsible for social encounters. Thus, spatial configuration is related to social order and social cohesion.

3.4.2 Space proxemics

Proximity means nearness in place and time (Oxford University Press, 2007). Proxemics is a term coined by E.T. Hall, which defines the interrelated observations and theories of man's use of space as a specialized elaboration of culture. Hall (1966) coined the term Proxemics from the Latin root prox- as in proximity and the suffix-emic as in systemic or phonemic. The term indicates the programmatic relationship of man with his immediate surroundings. It is the study of how man unconsciously structures micro space to conduct daily transactions. It is the way spaces in a house are organized and ultimately the layout of the towns. Hall (1966) has also observed that people in different cultures utilize space differently from one another. The branch of knowledge also deals with the amount of space that people feel it necessary to set between themselves and others.

Figure 3.2 Neighbourhood in Bay Area near San Francisco

Americans apparently direct attention more towards content than structure or form; the importance of culture is often minimized (Hall, n.d.). Figure 3.2 shows standardized and uniform structures in a neighbourhood in a Bay Area near San Francisco. In American built environment, less importance is always given to making physical appearance distinctive/appealing. In India, it is exactly opposite where there are significant implications of peculiar cultural values on the built environments.

The term 'proxemics' is extended at the city level, where it is used to define culture-specific user preferences about space utilisation. It can also be called as principles of urbanism specific to built environments in India. Spatial configuration which matches with the user preferences about space proxemics will reinforce the positive elements in social life. Non-congruence of user preferences about space proxemics and built environment results into conflicting situations in urban areas.

3.4.3 Physical determinism

Apart from the discussed theories by Amos Rapoport, Christopher Alexander and Bill Hillier, there are many theories about user–built-environment interface and socio-cultural aspects. In the study of user–built-environment interface, the theories are located somewhere along the continuum ranging between a deterministic definition of environment and one that minimizes impact of built environment on user.

According to social constructivism (Jacqueline, 2008), behaviour results from a learned social norms and is not influenced by the physical environmental context in which it occurs. In reality, certainly the users' behaviour is influenced not only by the space they occupy but also by their feelings, intensions, expectations and social context in which they are participating. At the same time, space offers certain obstructions and possibilities which influences users' behaviour.

A better understanding of how we are all affected by built environment is needed, and it pivots on the notion of use. In between the whole spectrum of theories between physical determinism and social constructivism, there lies somewhere in the middle the user-centric approach to study built environment (Fig. 3.3). And study of relationship of spatial cognition and configuration is part of user-centric approach for dealing built environments.

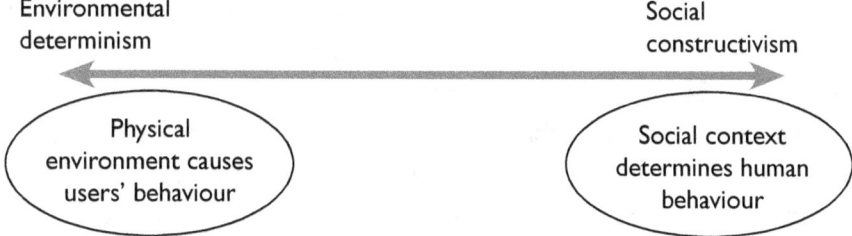

Figure 3.3 Spectrum of theories related to user–built environment relationship

Space is created not directly by the interrelated demands of specific activity patterns, but indirectly by the different demands that kinds of activities place on the movement and on co-presence that is created by space (Hillier, 2008)". Spaces do not totally determine usage pattern, but pattern of usage of spaces is different with different culture, thus demanding different pattern of spaces. Also the usage pattern of spaces leads to emergence of certain kind of built environments. Thus, the investigation is no way trying to emphasize physical determinism of the built environment, but it is trying to understand and make user-centric built environments.

3.5   Spatial configuration: Past, present and future

In the long history of city forms and shapes from western Asia, Mesopotamia to today's new towns, the science of geometry has played an outstanding role. Looking at the urban morphologies in past and present, one can find that in terms of geometries, there are two distinct typologies. One is the conventional geometry of straight lines known as Euclidean geometry and other is organic pattern. The organic pattern is usually not considered formally as planned and orderly.

Euclidian geometry was the main and powerful tool in the hands of planners and designers while attempting to arrive at spatial configuration and apply order to city forms. While Aristotle (c. 384–322 BC) contributed to the key ideas and concepts of understanding and classifying nature, Euclid (c.325–265 BC), in particular, established the geometrical principles and forms which dominated the history of architecture, city planning, and design – known as Euclidean geometry (www.fractalmorphology.com, n.d.). Orthogonality and grid have been an important tool in the hands of urban planners/designers for creating urban order. Looking at the successes that the geometry of straight lines has achieved through the history of urban forms, Kostof (1991, pp. 95–157) claims that the grid, in particular, has served human needs through the following purposes:

- Practical purposes of facilitating movement in working areas in city both for pedestrian and vehicular
- Political purposes of employing control
- Economical purposes, as it serves well the need for fast development in limited time and money
- Social purposes, as it serves for the equal distribution of land or the easy parceling and selling of real estate

Mostly the planning and design efforts from past to present are based on Euclidian geometry and orthogonality. The planned settlements or cities in Greek, Egyptian, and Roman or even in Indus Valley civilizations and also in late periods in historic times had used Euclidian geometry and grid Iron pattern. The influential idea of the grid-iron layout was developed by one of the first-known city planners, Hippodamus. He proposed a city plan that featured order and regularity, in contrast to the intricacy and complexity that were more common in earlier Greek cities, and he is called the originator of the idea that a town plan might formally embody and clarify a rational social order (Morris, 1979). The Romans moved on from Greek philosophy of geometry to practice. The influential work by Vitruvius developed the science of geometry to a more functional level at both architectural and urban scales. Urban historians (Mumford, 1961; Kostof, 1999), however, believe that the theories of absolute proportion lost their original significance in planning cities during the Middle Age. The classical theories of Euclidian geometry and proportions were revived and used extensively again in Renaissance period. According to Batty and Longley (1994, p.23), 'the need for regularity laid out city blocks, ideal town plans that were much more ambitious than anything previously'; and therefore, the Renaissance can be called 'the time of high theory for the city of pure geometry'. From the late 18th century onwards, it was the application of the pure grid-iron-based plan that became popular again in the planning of many rapidly growing European and American cities – except L'Enfant's plan for Washington DC which was claimed to be under the influence of Baroque planning layout (Mumford, 1961). The configurations derived out of Euclidian geometry had certain practical advantages. It facilitates easy and fast movement, especially vehicular movement. Also it is found suitable by administrators to employ control. It is suitable for fast development in case of limited time and resources. Thus, it is claimed to be an exceedingly flexible and diverse system of planning.

Historically, the grid served two main purposes. The first is to facilitate orderly settlement and colonization. Even in today's context, grid is rampantly used for real estate development and land speculation by developers in Indian developing cities. The other application of the grid has been as an instrument of modernization and of contrast to organic pattern that existed and was not considered as orderly. The virtue of the grid is precisely in being a conceptual formal order, non-hierarchical and neutral. However, with modernism came simplification and abstraction which have grossly compromised on the richness of depth and hierarchy. Hierarchies, as argued by Batty and Longley (1994), are basic organizing devices for describing and measuring the importance of urban functions across many spatial scales. As they are a property of general systems, their import extends beyond individual cities to systems of cities, and thus they present us with the framework for linking local to global and vice versa (Batty and Longley, 1994).

Our most recent understanding of urban structure recognizes a city to be a highly complex system, both in a static structural sense as well as in the dynamic sense of movement and continuous change (Salingaros, 2005). With time and use, even the planned cities with Euclidian geometry tend to show remarkable deviations from regular order to more complex configurations. Cities may sometimes start with sustained regular plans, but more commonly, their form involves continuous unpredictable processes of evolution over the time (Marshall, 2009). Figure 3.4 shows the transformation of a gridded Roman colony into an Islamic city due to order imposed by users over the period of time. It can be claimed that 'no two planned cities are exactly alike' (Kostof, 1999). As Batty and Longley (1994, p.2) explained, the reason is that 'even planned cities are adapted to their context in more natural ways once the plans come to be implemented'. This can prove that order as planned is not usually followed but users tend to impose their own order. Thus there is a need to evolve methods to understand and then, design user-centric built environments.

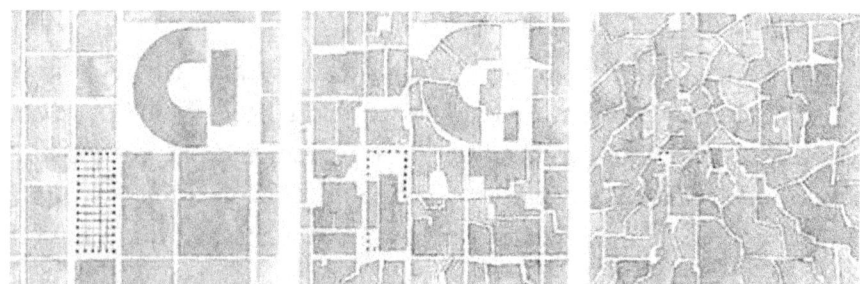

Figure 3.4 Gradual transformation of a gridded Roman colony into an Islamic city

This similar situation we find in most of the developing cities in India. The configurations are partially planned mostly with grid-iron pattern but with users imposing order, they tend to deviate from the formal regular configurations based on Euclidian geometry into more informal complex configurations depicting hierarchy and role of depth. It is true that the regular geometric configurations and the grid iron in particular have had some successes through the history and served human needs. At the same time, in an organically evolved configuration, as the order is not imposed by geometry but by users, they are more user friendly and humane. It is evolved gradually by decisions made by individual people (Kostof, 1999). Order embodies meaning, context and definition to the spatial arrangements and patterns developed by man to structure his activities (Kumar, 1998). Thus, the overriding factor about order in a spatial configuration of urban built environments is user preferences about space proxemics. Yet looking at the contemporary practices of designing built environments, one can realize that it has increasingly become a politically charged process as the 'society of the spectacle' becomes slowly realized in space (Cuthbert, 2003). In his recent essays on 'The Nature of Order', Alexander (2003, 2004) raises a very important point stating why the application of the conventional geometry as applied in planned cities creates 'mistakes'. In general, an organic structure emerges out of a generating process. The generating process – through iterated, repeated, sequence of transformations – makes it progressively 'more and more profound, more and more living' (Alexander, 2004, p.95). Thus, the configurations of urban systems need to be living self-organized systems and for that the process adopted for its evolution should change.

3.6   Concept of depth

Regarding urban areas, space syntax is based on the fact that the urban environment is an interconnected space where spaces link to other spaces (Long and Yixiang, 2007). In a built environment, there are unbuilt spaces in terms of linear spaces (roads) and convex spaces (urban open spaces), which form a system of spaces. The space syntax approach provides a way of looking urban morphology in terms of beaded ring system in which primarily linear spaces are narrow strings. At places, these widens into irregular beads. Based on this analogy of beaded ring, one can represent and understand system of spaces in urban environment.

In a syntactic analysis, the emphasis is on topological distance rather than metric distances. The depth is the basic and most important parameter of representing topological inter-relationships between spaces in a system of spaces. It means the minimum distance in terms of steps between two nodes. The quantification of relationships or configurations in terms of numerical parameters is based on the notion of topological distance or depth. The space syntax methodology rests on three basic conceptions of space: (a) isovist – the field of view from a particular point; (b) axial space – a straight line; and (c) convex space – a space where all points in space are physically and visually linked to all other points in the space. It means if a line is drawn between any two points in the space, it will not go outside the space. The concept of convex and axial space is shown in Fig. 3.5. The space syntax methodology with its techniques to deduce and quantify configurations cannot only help to understand its structure at one point of time but also helps to deduce generative rules so as to guide future transformations appropriately. The types of syntactic analysis include visual-field analysis, node analysis and axial-line analysis. In visual-field analysis, the spatial elements on which the calculation is based are 'visual-fields' or 'isovists'. Isovist means spaces where 'what you know is what you see'. For study of convex spaces, isovist analysis is more appropriate (Hillier, 1996; Hillier and Hanson, 1984). Visual-field analysis is often applied for studying spaces that are complex and overlapping but not 'street-alike'; for instance, public squares in cities and indoor space of buildings like museums or shopping malls. In node analysis, the space syntax model consists in a 'connectivity graph' of nodes and lines where the nodes usually represent a room, while the lines (or edges) represent connections between the spaces. Node analysis is particularly useful for studying dwellings since they usually consist of

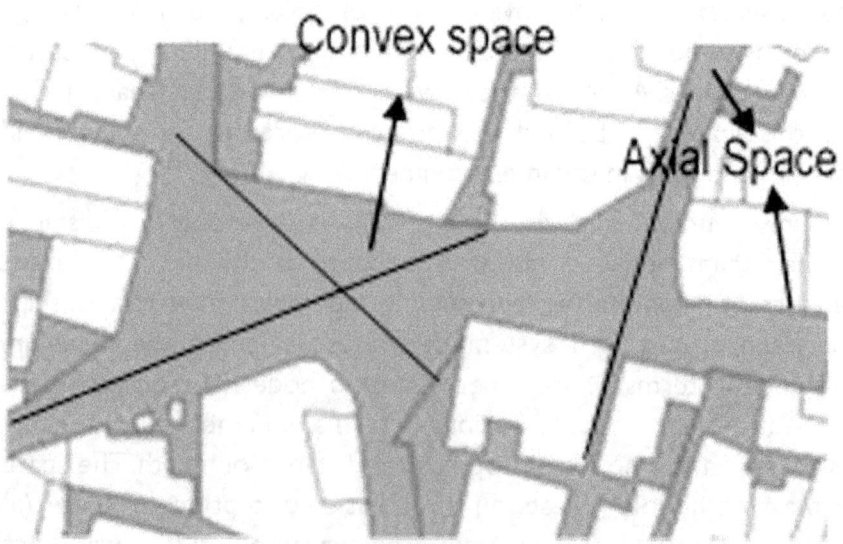

Figure 3.5 Convex and axial space

enclosed spaces (rooms) connected by doors or door-like openings. In axial-line analysis, the space is represented by straight lines, so-called axial lines. In brief, the space to be examined is modeled by 'fewest and longest straight lines covering all convex spaces' (Hillier and Hanson, 1984, pp. 91–92). Axial-line modelling captures basic features of continuous spaces such as the outdoor space between buildings in a city, a space that is a 'net' of long and intersecting 'street spaces'. Therefore, axial-line modelling is often applied in urban analysis. These axes are the representative lines of sight or visibility and movement or permeability. An axial map of the open space structure of the settlement will be the least set of such straight lines which pass through each convex space. Thus, space structure can be looked in terms of relation between axial and convex spaces as internal configurations and also in relation to world outside the system under consideration.

3.6.1 Axial-line modelling

The axial map is comprised of the fewest and the longest lines that cover all the available connections from one convex space to another. In other words, a set of axial lines that mutually intersect and cover a whole free space is called an axial map. Axial line is a form of unit space and describes physical and visual connections. Axial lines represent the longest views across spaces that capture the sense of what a person sees while moving in urban areas. On the other hand, it also represents a person's movement behaviour since people always walk in a straight line to minimize the distance, not a curved line. Thus, the axial lines simplify the complex urban environment and connect human spatial cognition and movement behaviour together (Long and Yixiang, 2007, p.43). Axial line model is a minimal set of lines that pass through the connecting roads within that system. The methodology to draw axial line map is as follows:

(a) Delineate area for axial maps by drawing a circle around area of interest and then take a radius of 30 min travel from edge (depends on mode of transport).
(b) Derive a map of spaces.
(c) Graphically represent the system of spaces in terms of axial map.

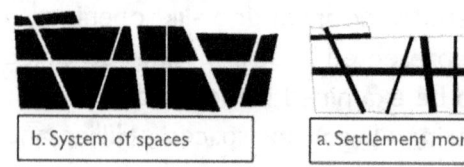 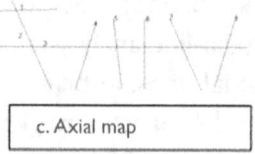

b. System of spaces   a. Settlement morphology   c. Axial map

Figure 3.6 Permeability graphs of lines 3 and 2

The methodology is illustrated with a part plan in Fig. 3.6.

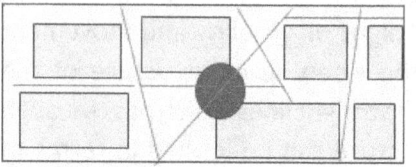 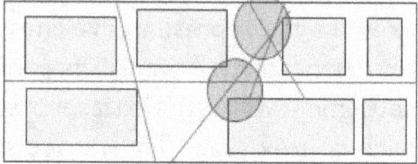

Figure 3.7 Axial lines in curved spaces

Figure 3.7 show incorrect ways of drawing axial map as the lines are neither fewest nor longest. Axial lines should connect entry and exit or one should document major movement pathways in open spaces through primary observations. In case of overpasses, bridges, subways, there is a way to unlink the axial lines as they are not linked. Curved linear spaces should be approximated by the smallest number of axial lines which match the space (Fig. 3.8). The analysis of axial map is based on graph theory. Space syntax describes the topological connections of unit spaces through depth analysis using the graph theory. Graph theory here means drawing a graph of each line in terms of its relations with the other lines, which is called a justified permeability graph. The justified permeability graphs of lines 1, 4, and 3, 2 are shown in Figs. 3.9 and 3.10.

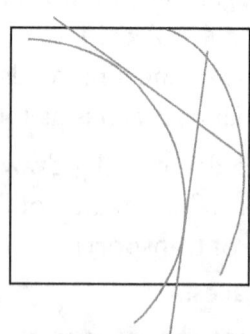

Figure 3.8 Axial map: Process

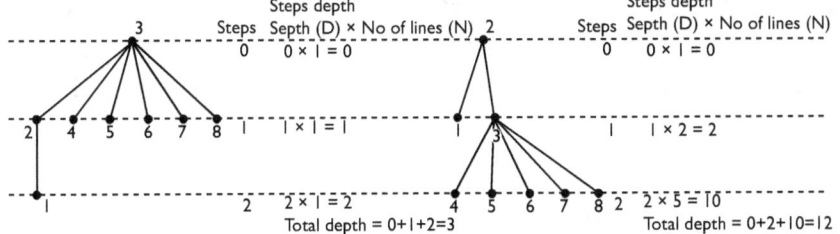

Figure 3.9 Axial map: Errors

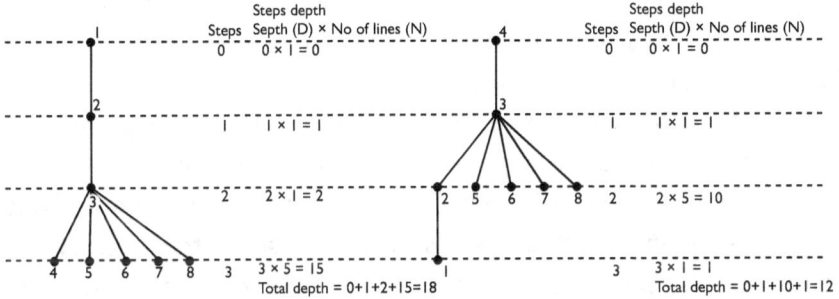

Figure 3.10 Permeability graphs of Lines 1 and 4

Based on these graphs, how each space is related to the other spaces can be described and calculated. The primary value that describes how one space is related to all the other spaces (topological relations) is total depth (TD). TD represents the number of turns (steps) that one needs to take to move from one space/line to another space/line. As a result, the topological graphs are transformed into numeric values, which objectively measure the spatial configuration. For each space/line, total depth could be calculated by averaging the depth in relation to each space/line in the urban space, which represents a global property. Besides the total depth, just several depths or steps could be calculated for each line. These relations between spaces are called a local property. More often researchers use up to 3 depths to represent the local properties between spaces since it generally covers a neighbourhood scale. Based on it, algorithms for calculating the other important syntactic properties such as global integration and local integration are being developed. By expressing the pattern/properties in a numerical way, we can find clear relations between space patterns and how collections of people use them (Hillier, 1996, p.22).

3.6.2 Applicability

While discussing about 'Indian built environment' and its peculiarity, Yatin Pandya has stated that continuity and linkages are important aspects of Indian built environments. According to Pandya (2004, p.30), there are innumerable nuances of traditional Indian built environment. Firstly, non-linear organization of spaces through shifting axis of movement helps gradually unfold spaces and introduce element of surprise (Fig. 3.11). Secondly, there are pause points and thresholds which help one reorient and reaffirm bearings in space. They are there in most of the Indian built environments but it is not enough to understand them as descriptions; instead, these should be quantified by specific mechanism. Hence, if one wants to understand Indian built environments, it necessitates understanding them as a system of spaces.

Figure 3.11 Shifting axis of movement

The important social space is street (that is linear or axial) in traditional Indian built environment, rather than defined convex spaces. Streets always acted as important community spaces and helped in maintaining social cohesion. Even in contemporary built environments, street appears to be evolving as an important social space where many religious, political, commercial and even recreational activities happen. 'Galli cricket campaign' by local television network is one example of using street as a recreational space. Spatial configuration can either encourage or discourage the use of street as community space. Figure 3.12 shows some photographs of use of street for religious, social, political or commercial activities. Therefore, axial-line modelling is identified as an approach for understanding the configurations of Indian built environment which can be inspected by representing the system of spaces through axial maps. There are number of softwares available for doing such type of syntactic analysis.

(d)

(d)

Figure 3.12 Use of street for religious, social, political or commercial activities

They are (Turner, 2007) as follows:

- Spatial Positioning Tool (SPOT) by H. Markhede, P. Miranda Carranza
- Webmap At Home by N. S. Dalton
- Confeego: Tool Set for Spatial Configuration Studies by J. Gil, C. Stutz, A. Chiaradia
- Syntax2D: An Open Source Software Platform for Space Syntax Analysis by J. Wineman, J. Turner, S. Psarra, S. K. Jung, N. Senske
- Segmen: A Programmable Application Environment for Processing Axial Maps by S. Iida
- Place Syntax Tool | GIS Software for Analyzing Geographic Accessibility with Axial Lines by A. Stoahle, L. Marcus, A. KarlstrÄom
- UCL Depthmap: From Isovist Analysis to Generic Spatial Network Analysis by A. Turner

After the study and exploring the use of few softwares, Depthmap4 by Bartlett School of Graduate Studies, UCL, London (User Guide – Annexure XIII) is identified and used for the study, as it is a multi-functioned, speed-optimized, stand-alone program for Windows 2000, XP or Vista (Turner, 2004).

3.6.3 Syntactic properties

For urban environments, an axial map gives the opportunity to objectively measure spatial configuration of the urban environment. There are three important syntactic measures of spatial configuration of an axial map: connectivity, local integration and global integration. The interpretive parameters are synergy and intelligibility. Connectivity is a measure of how well an axial line is intersected by other lines. Numerically, connectivity of a line is the number of lines getting connected to it. For example, a system of spaces with axial map is shown in Figs. 3.13 and 3.14. Since there are 2 axial lines (11, 0) directly intersecting axial line 1, connectivity of line 1 is 2. The length of an axial line has some correlation to connectivity. There are more possibilities for lengthy lines to be intersected by others (Jiang, 1998).

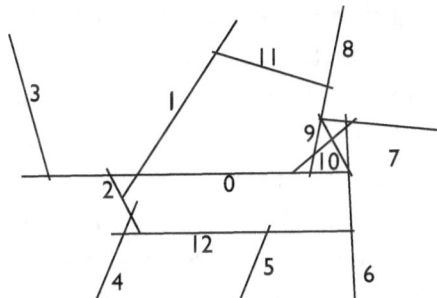

Figure 3.13 System of spaces and axial map

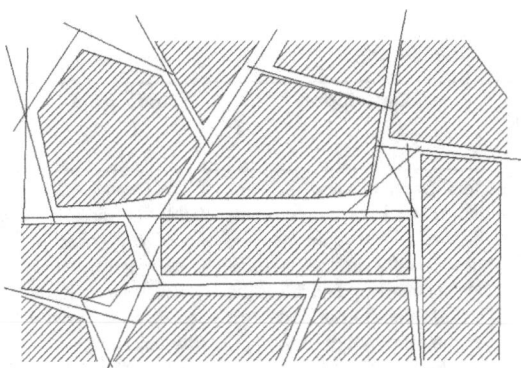

Figure 3.14 Axial map

A modification of connectivity is a control value that measures how each axial line controls access to immediate neighbors (i.e., those lines intersected by the current one). Both connectivity and control value are local measures since they only take into account relationships between a space and its immediate neighboring spaces (Jiang, 1998). Figure 3.13 shows an axial map using graduated color symbology based on the integration values. Graphic technique helps in visualization and comparison of spatial configuration of different systems. Generally, an accepted rule is to represent high global (>1.35) or local integration (>2.70) with red subsequent lower values with other warm colours such as orange, yellow and so on. Cool colors such as green display low global integration (0.86–1.02) and low local integration values (1.33–1.73). Shades of blue colour indicate further lower values: global integration (0.36–0.86) and local integration (0.33–1.33).

Integration of a line is a value that indicates the degree to which a line is more integrated or segregated from a system as a whole. Depth and connectivity of axial lines when moving from one space to all other spaces in the system will decide accessibility. A space is said to be integrated, when all other spaces of the urban environment are well connected from it. Thus integration is a function of depth, as more the depth the space will not be easily accessible. In this regard, integration is a measure of syntactical accessibility (Long and Yixiang, 2007, p.48). The steps for calculating integration values can be found in Table 3.1.

Table 3.1 Syntactic measures

Syntactic measure name/ parameter	Description	Indicators	Remarks
Mean depth	Total Depth of a node n, TD(n), is the total of the shortest distances from node n to the other nodes in the systems. Mean Depth for a node n is the average depth from node n to all the other nodes.	Mean Depth, MD = $L/(N-1)$ where, L = Total Depth (in terms of no. of steps) and N = total number of spaces in a system (Manum, 2009)	Very much a investigation number

Contd...

Contd...

Syntactic measure name/ parameter	Description	Indicators	Remarks
Relative Asymmetry	Relations of depth necessarily involves notion of asymmetry RA generalizes this by comparing	Relative Asymmetry $RA = 2(MD - 1)/(K - 2)$ where, MD = mean depth, K = no. of space in a system (Manum, 2009)	Lower value lesser depth more of integration
Real Relative Asymmetry	RA values can be used to compare various spaces of approximately same size. If one has to compare across systems which differ significantly in size, there is a need to take one more transformation to eliminate the effect of size.	Real Relative Asymmetry (RRA) = RA/X where, $X = [6.644K \cdot \log_{10}(K + 2) - 5.17K + 2]/(K \sim 3K + 2)$ (Khadiga and Mamoun, n.d.)	RA values are then adjusted between theoretical and empirical limits to allow direct comparisons across patterns regardless of their size. Known as the Real Relative Asymmetry (RRA)
Integration	Integration of a node is by definition expressed by a value that indicates the degree to which a node is integrated or segregated from a system as a whole (global integration), or from a partial system consisting of nodes a few steps away (local integration)	Integration = $1/RAA$ (Manum, 2009)	Low values indicate integration and high values indicate segregation
Connectivity	It denotes the number of immediate neighbourhoods of an axial line		The connectivity of an axial line measures the number of lines that directly intersect that given axial line

The higher the integration value of a line, the less its depth, which means the line has high syntactic accessibility in the system. The system of spaces can be read with different topological radii.

Hence, the integration can be of two types: local integration and global integration.

- If we are counting all nodes in the system, we could get global integration which represents correlation of a node with all other nodes in the system.

- If we are counting the nodes within a radius k, we can get local integration values characterizing the relationships between that node and the neighboring nodes within the search radius.
- Hillier has argued that pedestrian densities could best be understood by calculating the lines up to two lines away from each line (radius3 integration).
- Relating local and global integration, one can understand the relationship between parts and the whole.

Intelligibility is defined as a correlation between connectivity and global integration. It is an important indicator of how clear an urban system is for its users. Hillier defined intelligibility as 'the degree to which what can be seen and experienced locally in the system allows the large-scale system to be learnt without conscious effort' (Hillier, 1996, p.215). This means that if a person is moving in a layout of high intelligibility, he/she will understand the overall structure of the configuration. Intelligibility values can be used to quickly compare spatial configuration of different urban environments. If the intelligibility concept is compared with Lynch's legibility concept (Lynch, 1992), intelligibility indicates the ease with which its parts (landmarks, paths, districts, edges and nodes) can be recognized and can be organized into a coherent pattern. It is evident that both address clear or coherent configurational properties (Long and Yixiang, 2007, p.49). It is observed that depth minimizing form is far more intelligible than depth maximizing form (Hillier, 1996, p.247). Traditional built environments with organic order are mostly depth maximizing forms and hence obviously less intelligible. Study of traditional built environments can help us to understand the priorities in terms of depth gain as user preferences of segregating or integrating public and private domain.

Synergy is an indicator of part to whole relationship in a system. The key to understand parts and whole is the integration for different radii. Radius3 describes integration at neighbourhood level appropriately; hence, R3 is identified as local integration. Hence, local area effect is quantified by synergy; it is the relationship between local integration R3 and global integration Rn.

Based on the understanding of the parameters and the way they are calculated, the configuration in Fig. 3.13 is analyzed manually. The parameters are given in following Table 3.2.

Table 3.2 Parameters

Ref. no.	Connec-tivity	Step Depth	Total Depth	Node Count	Mean Depth	Integra-tion
0	6	0	19	13	1.58	2.59
1	3	1	26	13	2.16	1.29
2	3	1	24	13	2	1.51
3	1	1	30	13	2.5	1.01
4	2	2	28	13	2.33	1.13
5	1	3	37	13	3.08	0.727
6	5	1	20	13	1.66	2.27
7	4	2	25	13	2.08	1.39
8	5	1	23	13	1.91	1.65
9	4	2	25	13	2	1.39
10	5	1	21	13	1.75	2.02
11	2	2	30	13	2.5	1.20
12	3	2	26	13	2.16	1.29

3.7 Spatial cognition

Hart and Moore (1973, p.248) defined spatial cognition as 'the knowledge and internal or cognitive representations of the structure, entities, and relations of space'. In other words, it is the internalized reflection and 'reconstruction of space in thoughts'. It is the human understanding and perception of geographic space. There is another term always referred to: environmental cognition which indicates the human ability to imagine and think about the world around us. Environmental cognition is a broader term than spatial cognition, since it includes not only the human ability to understand and reconstruct environments, but also the ability to make plans and solve problems, such as route choice and way finding. Spatial cognition specifically refers to an urban environment and complex buildings (Downs and Stea, 1974). There is another term which is often used: environmental perception. According to Passini (Long and Yixiang, 2007, p.6), environmental perception is more related to 'sensory information', whereas environment cognition or recognition is considered 'memory information'.

3.7.1 Neurophysics

A new branch of cognitive studies called neurophysics deals with human brain activity, sense, perception and memory, entirely from physics point of view. It gives detail analysis of audio-visual perception and memory in terms of electromagnetic frequencies with the well-established recordings of electroencephalography (EEG). When we say perception or mental images, the brain is not having picture-like images stored. Nevertheless, all kinds of the sensory information are stored in the form of electromagnetic radiations and we call it as memory. According to Narendra Katkar (2012), since childhood, humans are creating a self-imposed embedded program through juxta-positioning descriptive audio-induced (language) signals with visual light produced signal in the center of brain, and these reactivate as memory. It is found that frequency codes are in zero state in early life and infancy. As we grow, develop and mature, number of frequency codes are constantly recorded which we call as developing memory. This information is then structured in a certain manner which we call cognitive map and retrieved as and when required. Whenever new information is recorded, it is compared with already recorded information. If there is mismatch or discrepancy in the recorded information and the new information, there is a confusion and conflict. Due to common, socio-economic, cultural background and similar physical setting in which a community/society lives, they tend to have similar information coded over the period. Hence, there are some commonalities about the way members of society develops spatial cognition. Thus, different cultures have different space time concepts, different views of reality and different ways of defining places and giving meaning/ importance, which results in peculiarities in spatial cognition and subsequently culture-specific user preferences about space proxemics.

3.8   Cognitive mapping

Spatial cognition is subfield of environmental psychology. Cognitive mapping is a process composed of a series of psychological transformations by which individual acquires, stores, recalls and decodes information about the relative locations and attributes of the phenomena in his everyday spatial environment (Downs and Stea, 1974). In more general terms, the act of cognitive mapping is 'the mental structuring process leading to the creation of a cognitive map'. A cognitive map may be defined as 'an overall mental image or representation of the space and layout of a setting'. Cognitive map is the term used to refer to one's internal representation of the experienced world (Wikipedia contributors, 2012b). In reality, investigators in different fields may use different terms such as mental maps, mental image, and mental pictures, which have the same meaning as cognitive maps (Downs and Stea, 1974). Cognitive maps are invariably incomplete and partially distorted features that can be revealed in external representations or in spatial behaviours.

Edward Tolman (1948) inferred for the first time the existence of cognitive maps by recording the spatial behaviour of a maze-running rat who took a 'short cut' to the final destination by running across the top of a maze instead of following a route through it. The term 'cognitive mapping' has been used in three different ways (Kitchin and Freundschuh, 2000, p.2). First, as a descriptive title for the field of study that investigates how people learn, remember and process spatial information about an environment. Second, it is used as phrase for the process of thinking about spatial relations. Third, it has been used as a descriptive name for a methodological approach to understand cognition in general. Here cognitive mapping is referred to as methodological approach and cognitive map as a person's spatial knowledge of the immediate environment.

Spatial knowledge or knowledge of a place is the essential part of cognitive map. Cognitive map may or may not have map-like form. Cognitive map does include not only the observable physical environment but also the many varied social and cultural environments that impinge and affects behaviour (Stokols and Altman, 1987). Cognitive maps are used to understand and know the environment, predict the environment, and guide spatial behaviour (such as wayfinding) in the environment. Such knowledge is explicitly spatial but it may also be non-spatial and culturally coded in terms of symbolism, values, and beliefs and so on. Hence, it is basically the information structured regardless of physical form/manifestation and obviously varies due to values, \beliefs and cultural background. Three important components of a cognitive maps are places, spatial relations and travel plans (Stokols and Altman, 1987). Stea and Downs (1974) have indicated that cognitive maps also reflect information about the hierarchical arrangement of points in space, with respect to relative distance and size. Thus, the planning aspects of built environment in terms of configuration and hierarchies have significant relationship with spatial cognition. Urban planners such as Lynch and Appleyard have stressed on the importance of spatial configuration in spatial cognition (Appleyard, 1976). The intended investigation tries to understand relationship of cognition and configuration in India.

3.8.1 Spatial knowledge

The important component of cognitive map is spatial knowledge structure. The spatial knowledge structure of a cognitive map consists of locational information of places, its relational information and configurational or topological information which guides the spatial decision making or behaviour in terms of travel plans. Thus, spatial knowledge structure or cognitive map has places, spatial relations and travel plans (behaviour decisions). The spatial relations between spaces in terms of locational, relational, configurational leads to formation of cognitive map. Relational knowledge builds on locational knowledge and is about distances and directions. Configurational knowledge about an environment accumulates over a period due to locational and relational knowledge as the notions about proxemics get embedded into it. For us to understand, user preferences in terms of space proxemics, the configurational knowledge of cognitive map is most important.

Landmarks and edges are important aspects of locational information of places. The cognition or cognitive mapping is not only about places in terms of landmarks and nodes but also about their relative locations and connectivity. A critical component of relative location or relational information of cognitive map is spatial separation and is known by the term cognitive distance or subjective distance. Distance is really often a milieu within which a variety of behaviours and phenomena occur. Subjective distance can be in terms of metric distance, time or cost. Briggs showed that cognitive distance is a function of both the city structure and the behaviour by which the structure is learnt (Downs and Stea, 1974, p.387).

It's not just the characteristics of places or their relative positions which make them identifiable; however, their configurational aspects certainly come into picture. Following the Lynch's work, Appleyard (1976) conducted investigation in Venezuela identifying reasons for certain nodes or landmarks getting incorporated into cognitive images. According to him, though buildings are known for their characteristics such as intensity of use, community significance, level of visibility and so on, there is also a significant role played by their topological, positional and configurational characteristics.

Locations, distance between them and their configuration all are important components of cognitive map. Spatial configuration plays an important role in development of cognitive map. Travel plans or spatial behaviour is one effective way of understanding about individual's spatial cognition or cognitive map. Spatial knowledge or cognitive map is individual; however, that knowledge components can be shared or commonly agreed on in a group of people with common cultural background. Thus, culture consists of shared meanings, images and habits of a group and provides the conceptual matrix for commonalities in cognition. This aspect of cognition is what being referred by Rapoport as anthropological. It is about imposing order or giving meaning to the environment around.

Based on the structuring of all kinds of environmental information throughout, cognitive maps develop. According to Haq (2001), there are two ways in which environmental information is communicated to shape human cognitive maps. One is direct communication with the physical environment. Another is indirect representations of it, by being exposed to various media verbally and orally, such as direction maps, pictures, or moving images. More the exposure better will be the cognitive map and hence familiarity with the environment is important to human cognitive mapping development. Many recent studies in the field of cognition have concluded that cognition gets developed primarily by acting in space, i.e moving in space and using it. The way society uses space is cognition in anthropological sense. Daily use of the environment, for example the immediate surrounding or neighbourhood, will lead to formation of a good cognitive map of it. Individual's ability to comprehend the information will certainly affect the development of cognitive map, but since the investigation is focusing on anthropological aspect of cognition where society tries to impose order, the individual ability and competence is outside the discussion of this study. Understanding the movement pattern and spatial behaviour can help us to understand the way society imposes order on the built environment in terms of cognitive constructs as user preferences.

Abstraction is one important aspect of development of cognitive map. Visual qualities in terms of distinctiveness/homogeneity and imageability play an important role in development of cognition. Certain environmental elements, which are more 'imageable' than others, are easily stored in the human mind. As early as the 1960s, from interviewing and studying sketch maps of 36 residents in three American cities, Kevin Lynch suggested five key 'imageable' elements that comprise cognitive maps of urban settings: path, nodes (path intersections), landmarks, district, and edges (boundaries). After Lynch's pilot study, many studies (Appleyard and Lintell, 1972; De Jonge, 1962; Nasar, 1990; Gulick, 1963) have confirmed the results, but varying in importance of elements.

These cognitive representations are a subjective evaluation of the urban environment. They are extremely difficult to describe objectively. As stated by Gärdenfors (2004), the central problem for cognitive studies is how representations should be modeled. Their characteristics are hard to formulate, and they vary for different persons due to each person's varying cognitive systems. For example, Appleyard (1976) had proposed the size of the building to be an important characteristic of a landmark, while Evans (1980) had suggested color as an important characteristic. Appleyard (1969) synthesized the characteristics of urban elements that make them recognizable as landmarks into five major categories. The categories include: use (function), location, historical meaning, physical characteristics and maintenance. Landmarks, nodes and districts are usually referred to discrete elements and use, historical meaning, building features are their properties. Locations of these discrete elements are relational properties (Haq, 2001), which depend on spatial configuration and will have importance while discussing cognition in anthropological sense. Discrete elements and their properties are important for psychological aspect of cognition.

3.8.2 Socio-economic and cultural aspects of cognition

Socio-economic and cultural aspects do have implications on cognition. Culture refers to a body of knowledge and beliefs that is more or less shared between individuals within a group and transmitted across generations (Montello, 1995). Essentially, culture specifies preferred or accepted patterns of ideation and behaviour dealing with religious and value systems, and material/technological systems. Cognition deals with knowledge: its acquisition, storage, retrieval, manipulation and use by organisms or machines to achieve behavioural goals. Defined in this broad and theoretically neutral way, cognition includes structures and processes involved in perception, learning, thinking, memory, reasoning and problem solving and language. Spatial cognition refers to these structures and processes when they deal with spatial knowledge: knowledge of location (including distance and direction) size, shape and pattern as well as changes in these properties across time.

Some aspects of cognition are universal irrespective of culture-related differences due to the fact that all humans have similar nervous system, similar body structure and learning, socialization similarities. Also the environment is similar in terms of enduring regularities of physical world such as its 3-dimensionality, gravitation and earth's structure, pattern of rotation, cardinal directions. However, there are many aspects of spatial cognition which are different in different cultures and which have effect on spatial configuration and behaviour.

The reasons of culture-related differences in spatial cognition stated by Montello (1995) include:

1. Due to cultural differences, there is a different spatial language which is based on relationship of language and thought.
2. Pictorial perception is different in different cultures. Some traditional cultures have minimal or restricted prior experience with the conventions of pictorial representation, though it is unlikely that any human group does not practice some iconic pictorial representations. In Indian culture, pictorial representations of spatial relationships are not very common.
3. Different culture practice different forms of economic activity; this entails among other things different temporal and spatial patterns of activity.
4. Lastly, spatial cognition is in the environmental features or cues that are noticed, remembered and verbally labelled. As environments differ with respect to cultures, obviously what one sees and remembers will also differ for people with different cultural backgrounds.

Age, gender, social and economic class are important social aspects. Familiarity, occupation and commutability in terms of workplace location and mode of travel are other important aspects which have a role to play in cognition.

Some of the researchers have focused on investigating age, gender and class differences, familiarity, commutability and resultant differences and cognition. Appleyard (1976) found that men drew slightly more accurate and extensive city maps than women did, which he attributed to greater travel and exposure in the city by men. Professionals involved in the field of architecture and engineering obviously tend to have better cognition. In addition, some studies investigated effect of class differences on cognition. Appleyard (1976) found in his investigation in Ciudad Guyana, Venezuela, that Low-class people had better cognition than the upper class. Appleyard suggested that the greater knowledge of lower class was explained by their daily travel experiences. The poor travelled across town each day to the variety of work places. Thus the poor gained wider city exposure. Several researchers have examined the effects of setting familiarity on spatial cognition by comparing residents and strangers. Familiarity is the amount of exposure between an individual and the urban environment that they use (Long and Yixiang, 2007). Principles of commutability mean an inhabitant's daily commuting experiences which depend mostly on workplace location and mode of transport.

Appleyard (1976) found significant correlation with mode of travel, which in turn was correlated to class. Though bus riders generally saw more of the city, but had a poorer cognition due to lack of personal involvement in decision making. Users when move in slow traffic or when move as pedestrians, there is more time and chance to perceive the environment and hence have better cognition.

The aim of the investigation is to understand relationship between spatial configuration and spatial cognition to understand user preferences. The focus is on anthropological aspect of cognition and hence the investigation is not focusing on spatial cognition of individual but society with common cultural background. Within the considered group, the user groups whose cognition is to be studied should be homogeneous with respect to age, gender, social class (family size and economic class) and mode of travel. Also there should not be any professionals such as architects, which by training have better spatial cognition. These factors are considered while identifying respondents for surveys conducted to understand cognition of users.

3.8.3 Externalization of cognitive map

As stated already, the process of acquiring the spatial knowledge is denoted as the cognitive mapping process. The product, the sum total of environmental information stored in memory is called cognitive map. Although not strictly cartographic, a cognitive map experientially contains some map-like qualities. The development of cognitive map is mostly through direct communication with the physical environment except in some cases, where it is through indirect representations such as direction maps, pictures or moving images.

There are various methods discussed and used by number of researchers, and some of them are as follows (Jiang, 1998):

- Asking subjects to introspect by Binet in 1894
- Through maze learning by Tolman in 1932
- Sketch map advocated by Lynch in 1960
- Sketch map procedures and some resulting topological clustering to classify/categories by Appleyard in 1969
- Use of toys and games with children by Blaut in 1970
- Inter-point subjective distance judgment by Briggs in 1972
- Recognition tests about city scenes by Milgram in 1972
- Combined scaling and category grouping methods to obtain judgments of inter-point proximities by Golledge and Spector in 1976
- Judging locations and objects by Farrah in 1977
- Estimations of length of streets and angles of intersections by Byrne in 1979
- Subjects to interact with a computer in order to develop configuration of places by Baird in 1979
- Photos of places and locations to be placed on map board by Rayner in 1980

The search for most appropriate way to represent stored information in form of cognitive map is quite crucial. Developmental difficulties in spatial abilities and differences in verbal and drawing skills always interfere in externalizing internal spatial structure (Stokols and Altman, 1987). Sketch map is often used by researchers. Sketch map assumes that a person understood the abstract representative notion of a map and its relation to the real world. Also he/she is capable of translating spatial information from large to small scales.

Spatial aptitude or expertise varies with profession. Common man with average or no spatial aptitude will have difficulty in using sketch map to externalize his/her cognitive constructs. In India, the appropriateness of sketch map as a process to understand about cognition is questionable. In Indian context, it's observed that the cartographic understanding is very poor. People are not used to comprehending, using or drawing visual representations of built environments around in the form of maps. Here, the following statement holds true. 'We easily recognize configurations without conscious thought and just as easily use configurations in everyday life without thinking of them, but we do not know what is it we recognize and we are not conscious of what it is we use and how we use it' (Hillier, 1996). Hence other methods such as behaviour maps, recognition tests and questionnaire surveys are considered to externalize the cognition and are discussed in detail in methodology.

3.9   Syntactic analysis for cognition studies

Movement which is to an extent determined by spatial configuration is the fundamental attribute for spatial experience and subsequently spatial cognition. Spatial configuration is not only the driving force for human activity within urban environments, but it certainly influences human cognition and further determines human activity within urban environments since spatial cognition is shaped by movement within spaces (Jiang, 1998). So as shown in Fig. 1.6, spatial cognition and configuration are very much related and interdependent. Spatial cognition has two important aspects: anthropological and psychological. Previous literature in spatial cognition also revealed that an individual's first and primary spatial cognition is based on topological information, not metric information (O'Neil, 1991). Hence, understanding the relationship between spatial configuration and spatial cognition is important to understand configuration in terms of topology. Metric distance and depth are two important factors in spatial cognition. It is found that depth becomes more influential than metric distance as the spatial scale of cognition expands (Long, Baran and Robin, 2007). Space syntax describes the topological relationships of spatial configuration rather than metric distances and allows rigorous analysis of building and city structures that is both theoretical and mathematical (Long and Yixiang, 2007). Haq (2001) has also argued, 'Space syntax does seem to be a useful theory and methodology for understanding the role of environmental form from the point of view of topological relations in the study of environmental cognition and human wayfinding behaviour' (p.64). Thus, the syntactic analysis based on the notion of depth is considered for the undertaken study.

Various researchers have used space syntax in study of relationship of spatial configuration and spatial cognition. Space syntax approach to study spatial configuration and spatial cognition was used for the first time by Peponis, Zimiring and Choi in 1990. They investigated cognition and wayfinding performance in a complex hospital by using space syntax techniques. Later Haq (1999) used a similar methodology in a larger and more complicated urban hospital. He found integration as an important syntactic parameter for making choice of paths to be used. Kim (2001) conducted a study to understand the relationship between configuration, cognition and behaviour. He found strong correlations between axial integration in residents' sketch maps and axial integration of the real map. Also, correlations were found between sketch map integration and observed movement. Lay (2005) investigated the relationships between spatial configuration, spatial behaviour and spatial cognition using space syntax approach. He used various approaches to measure spatial cognition other than sketch map which included questionnaires, and behaviour maps to document people's spatial behaviour. Yun and Kim (2007) investigated the interrelationship between spatial cognition and configuration, and the effects of turns in path (depth) and metric distance in forming spatial cognition by using space syntax. They found that there is a strong interrelationship between the syntactic properties and spatial cognition as indicated in the cognitive map. In the investigation, a comparison of the influence of depth and that of distance showed that depth has more influence than distance on spatial cognition.

In 2007, Yixiang Long has done an investigation on 'The Relationships Between Objective and Subjective Evaluations of the Urban Environment: Space Syntax, Cognitive Maps, and Urban Legibility'. The study focuses on exploring the relationships between human cognitive representations and spatial configuration of the urban environment and the effects that different spatial configurations have on legibility of the environment. The space syntax approach was utilized to measure spatial configuration of the neighbourhoods. Sketch maps, recognition tests and interviews were used to measure individuals' cognitive representations and their perceived legibility of the environment. Overall, the results of the correlation study indicated that there exists a positive association between cognitive representation and spatial configuration.

Space syntax thus utilizes the powerful resources of graph theory and matrix algebra to tackle various problems in planning and design with great flexibility (Osman and Suliman, 1996). Yet after more than two decades of its publication, its validity remains controversial. It is mostly due to limited exploration by architects. The most noted review is the criticism of Low and Lawrence (1990), which briefly outlines the inadequacy of the technique, as it exists, in projecting society's norms. Similar remarks were made by social science scholar Edmund Leach (1978). He argued that the syntactic argument is meaningful and interesting, but he does not believe that one can immediately infer the generative syntax simply by looking at the layout of settlement patterns on the ground, and even if one could be sure of what the generative syntactic rules have been, one cannot infer anything at all about the society that makes use of the resultant settlement. It's accepted that 'without knowing the facts,' a two-dimensional plan of system of spaces in a built environment is an insufficient source for inferring social order or user preferences.

Nevertheless, it's a powerful tool which can be used for an analysis with support of primary data in terms of ground realities. Hence, the undertaken investigation is using space syntax as a tool, and the study is substantially supported by the primary data collected regarding spatial cognition of users.

3.10   Indian context

There are very few researchers in the field of spatial cognition or perception of urban environment in Indian context except by Kalapa Markandey (1997). Similar concern is also expressed by Jadon (2007) where he states that primary investigation studies in the field of image perception in Indian cities are marginal. He has mentioned few professionals who have discussed the issue. The list includes his studies about concepts of urban space, serial vision and skyline within the walled city of Delhi. Dongre (1992) has explored image perception within a small Indian town as a database towards planning process. Shirodkar (2005) has analysed transformations of specific streetscapes of Goa over a historical period of time. He has also expressed the similar concern in terms of superimposing western concepts of urban planning and theories without acknowledging ground realities of socio-cultural patterns and racial differences in perception in case of India. In the investigation, Markandey explored the role of spatial cognition in spatial behaviour. According to her, mental images of social proximity and physical distance interact to produce a response in terms of behaviour.

As far as syntactic analysis in case of built environments in India is concerned, an important study is by Shibu Raman (2003). Raman (2003) studied the relationship between culture and space in Indian context, specific to Ahmedabad. He has argued that a culturally sensitive design approach could help in attaining a diverse but cohesive society, thus achieving a socially sustainable urban community. His study examines the differences in morphology of different areas of the walled city of Ahmedabad, where different ethnic communities live in distinct localities. This analysis was carried out by using space syntax methodology. Different localities within the walled city were studied, both as they are embedded in the city and in isolation. The investigation showed many similarities in the local areas of Ahmedabad in terms of their syntactic values and the structuring principles of spaces. However, a detailed analysis showed some differences in the spatial patterns of Hindu and Muslim communities. These differences when looked at in conjunction with the ethnic landscape of the city revealed some interesting aspects of typical social and cultural patterns of the walled city of Ahmedabad.

3.10.1 Space proxemics in India

The reasons for peculiarities about user preferences of space proxemics are due to cultural and economic background. The cognitive constructs about structuring time are different as Indian society in general is polychronic in nature.

Spatial cognition can be termed as culture-specific constructs about structuring space, time and distance in a built environment. There are two contrasting ways of handling time: monochronic and polychromic (Hall, 1966). Monochronic is characteristic of low involvement society, who compartmentalizes time and spaces. They usually tend to schedule time to do one thing at a time. Instead, polychronic society with too much of involvement with each other, tend to keep several operations/activities going on at same time. Spatial segregation of activities works well in society with monochronic attitude. However, the polychronic attitude results into preference for pattern of mixed activities and emergence of informal activities in built environments.

Firstly, Indian society by and large is polychronic. Secondly, in Indian built environments, street acts as an important social space rather than demarcated community open spaces. Thirdly, there are peculiarities about structuring distance or subjective distance due to the mixed modes of transportation. In Indian society, the cognition is developed due to slow-moving traffic, either two-wheeler or pedestrian movement. Even the modern built environments are trying to accommodate the needs of automobile, yet the users usually use it as if they are walking.

This understanding about cognitive constructs in terms of user preferences about space proxemics, in case of Indian built environments, may help for better congruence between subjective and objective morphology. It will help to reduce the conflicting situations in built environment in India.

3.10.2 Street as a social space

The street, in addition to being a physical element in the city, is a social factor. It can be analyzed in terms of who owns uses and controls it, the purpose for which it was built, and its changing social and economic functions. It also has a three-dimensional form. The street provides a link between buildings both within the street, and in the city at large (Moughtin, 1992, p.131). Street is a physical and social part of the living environment and is used simultaneously for vehicular movement, social contacts and civic activities. This has long been argued by many authors including Kevin lynch, Donald Appleyard, Jane Jacobs and Southworth and Ben-Joseph (1997). Street patterns contribute significantly to the quality and character of a community. The number of blocks, intersections, access points and loops of cul-de-sacs per unit area affect the number of route options and ease of moving about.

Location advantages/disadvantages in terms of exposure due to visual and physical linkages, i.e. configuration, play an important role in proliferation of formal and informal activities on/along streets which tend to make them social spaces. Thus, while designing built environments, one should consider this. In the countries such as the Netherlands, Germany, England, Australia, Japan and Israel, the integration of traffic and residential activity in the same spaces has simulated new design configurations that increase social interaction and safety on the street and promote pedestrian movement (Southworth and Ben-Joseph, 1997, p.109). In India, there is a need to first understand the role of configuration in emergence of streets as social spaces and then evolve appropriate designs for such streets.

3.11 Spatial design

Wikipedia defines spatial design as a 'relatively new discipline that crosses the boundaries of traditional design disciplines such as architecture, interior design, landscape architecture and landscape design' ('Spatial design,' 2012). As defined by Cuthbert (2003) urban planning is a design of spatial arrangement of the activities and objects over an extended area, where the client is multiple, the programme is indeterminate and control is partial. Urban design (Cuthbert, 2003) is a part of city planning which deals with aesthetics and which determines the order and form of the city. In spatial design, the emphasis of the discipline is upon working with people and space, particularly looking at the notion of place, also place identity and genius loci (the spirit of a place). As such the discipline covers a variety of scales, from detailed design of interior spaces to large regional strategies.' Spatial design is at the interface of planning and architecture design. The task of city designer is to understand and express in built environment the needs and aspirations of the city group (Moughtin, 2003, p.12). In real world, all data have spatial reference. Spatial analysis has something to do with deriving information from data using its spatial context. The method widely used for spatial design is based on spatial analysis and spatial modelling. Generally, a model is a simplified description of reality, and modelling can be considered as a process of describing the reality. It can be a static reproduction or conceptual description.

3.11.1 Spatial modelling

Urban models are representations of functions and processes which generate urban spatial structure in terms of land use, population, employment and transportation. These are usually embodied in computer programs that enable location theories to be tested against data and predictions of future location patterns to be generated. A data model is an abstraction of the real world that employs a set of data objects that support map display, query, editing and analysis. It is the premeditated way to organize and display the information of urban reality in a spatial database (Putra, 2003).

The aim of spatial modelling is to derive a meaningful representation of events, occurrences or processes by making use of the power of spatial analysis. Models are simplifications of reality, theoretical abstractions that represent systems in such a way that essential features crucial to the theory and its application are identified and highlighted. In this role, models act as a vehicle to enable experimentation with theory in a predictive sense, and to enhance understanding which may be prior to predictions of situations as yet unrealized, for example, in the future (Batty, 2009).

Urban modelling is the process of identifying appropriate theory, translating into a mathematical or formal model, developing relevant computer programs and then confronting the model with data. It is worth noting that urban models span both theory and practice and their rationale depends on developing new theory as well as their use in policy making and planning. Here, a cognitive approach to spatial modelling of built environments in urban India means a process of describing and then dealing the reality of situations in urban India, based on the understanding of cognitive constructs or user preferences for space proxemics.

3.12   Summary

The evolution of spatial configurations in the past has been mostly based on science of geometry. In terms of geometries, there are two distinct typologies. One is the conventional geometry of straight lines – known as Euclidean geometry and other is organic pattern. Euclidean geometry was the main and powerful tool in the hands of planners and designers while attempting to arrive at spatial configuration and apply order to city forms. The configurations derived out of Euclidian geometry with orthogonality and gridded patterns had certain practical advantages. At the same time in an organically evolved configurations, as the order is not imposed by geometry but by users, they are more user friendly and humane. Hence, there is a need to think about the kind of spatial configurations we need to evolve and the method to be adopted for its evolution.

Not geometry but the topology with concept of depth is found central in understanding configurations. Hence to understand configurations in terms of depth distances, space syntax is identified as an analytical tool that can be used to quantify the topological relations within an urban built environment. This makes it an important tool in cognitive studies, since the evidence from spatial cognition studies has pointed to the importance of topological relationships in comprehension of a built environment. In Indian context, linear spaces are more important as social spaces than convex spaces and hence axial line modelling was chosen as a method of syntactic analysis. For studying the relationship of spatial configuration and cognition, space syntax methodology is used by many researchers.

Spatial cognition is abstract and internalized subjective expression of structures, entities, relations of space. Since childhood, human beings create a self-imposed program through juxta-positioning audio and visual signals in the brain. This information is then structured in a manner which we call cognitive map. Due to common socioeconomic cultural background and common setting in which society lives, a similar information is filtered and coded, stored in brain which results in peculiarities in spatial cognition and culture-specific user preferences about space proxemics. Cognition in anthropological sense is important for intended investigation, and it primarily develops through use of spaces. The travel plans as important aspect of cognition can be understood through behaviour maps.

Socioeconomic, cultural aspects such as age, gender, class differences, familiarity and commutability affect spatial cognition. Neighbourhood is at the interface of relationship of a house to the city. Though it's a physical entity, it is a cognitive construct.

The user–built-environment interface studied w.r.t varied built environments throughout the world highlighted that values affect subjective attitudes and many of these get manifest in built environment. Cities are historical products not only in their physical materiality but also in their cultural meaning and in the role they play in the social organizations and values. City design is one of the fundamental process through which historical actors have structured society according to their interest (Manuel, 2003, pp. 23–24). Since design and planning is primarily an act of decision making about spatial configuration, planners/designers need to creatively resolve inherent conflicts in user–environment interface. For that there is a need to understand culture-specific user preferences/attitudes for using built environment. An approach based on spatial cognition can help in developing this understanding. The term of space proxemics by E.T. Hall found suitable to describe culture-specific use of spaces. The term has been extended at the city level where it is used to describe culture-specific user preferences. These can be called as principles of urbanism in Indian context and used for modelling contemporary built environments. Spatial configuration if designed in congruence with cognitive constructs as user preferences about space proxemics, it will reinforce a positive element in social life.

Chapter 4

Photo: Entrance Gateway, Old Bhopal
By: Monali Jaiswal

Chapter 4

User preferences and traditional Indian settlements

Abstract: Traditional built environments appear much more humane and cohesive not only in India but also in many parts of the world, as they have evolved gradually and the user preferences got embedded into it. To understand traditional Indian built environments, it is important to quantify its spatial configuration in terms of system of spaces. This chapter is about the syntactic analysis of system of spaces in traditional built environments in India. The derived peculiarity of the built environment is compared with built environments from other parts of the world. The study has helped to derive cognitive constructs as user preferences in traditional Indian settlements.

Key words: Integration, connectivity, synergy, intelligibility, cognitive constructs

4.1 Significance

The way spaces are configured or arranged or patterned in a system of spaces can be called as spatial configuration. To understand traditional Indian built environments, it is important to quantify its spatial configuration in terms of system of spaces. Figure 4.1 shows a system of spaces in the traditional urban core of Varanasi. The concept of natural movement is central to system of spaces in a organically evolved built environment. It was believed till very recent past that spaces or spatial configuration in a built environment emerge due to functional requirements. As already discussed, natural movement is a fundamental corelate of the way spatial configuration is shaped. Thus, the traditional built environments have evolved over a period of time due to user preferences about movement and use of spaces. They have evolved as a result of a process of natural selection. Hence, by analysing spatial configurations of traditional built environments, one can understand the cognitive constructs in terms of user preferences rooted in it.

Figure 4.1 Spatial configuration: Traditional urban core (Varanasi)

The specific investigation question is intended with the need of understanding traditional built environments in terms of their configuration, as a result of user preferences. The chapter focuses on two questions: (1) How to understand and quantify the spatial configurations of organically evolved built environments of urban cores in Indian cities? (2) Based on the configuration parameters, can one understand the cognitive constructs in terms of intentions/preferences about spatial configurations of Indian cities?

4.2 Traditional built environments

The traditional Indian settlements though established at a point in space and time, they evolved in physical pattern as society evolved. Irregularity is the primary feature of organic cities as it cannot be measured in geometric properties such as repetition, symmetry, parallel elements, and alignment and so on. There is a difference between order and structure. Structure is the relationship between parts and the whole. An order results due to some principles based on generally accepted notion of sameness, repetition, geometry, grid, rhythm, symmetry and harmony. Geometrical properties help us to find out order but structure is about the relationship between parts and whole. These cities though lack in any obvious geometric order but certainly have structure. For analysing the system of spaces with focus on kinaesthetic quality and spatial structure, it is not only the geometry of spaces is important but more important is the topology. The relationship between the spaces and relationship of individual spaces to the whole system can only be understood through the concept of topology. Geometry is the way of representing the physical organisation, but it is not the creator of urban life, nor the logic behind its behaviour (Karimi and Kayvan, 1997). Hence these organically evolved parts of settlements need to be analysed to find out spatial structure within and the imposed order in terms of the way people use it.

As stated in Secction 1.1.1, the built environments in India are multilayered due to intense political, religious and cultural experiences throughout the history. What is existing today is out of the process of natural selection. Hence, it can be said that these spatial configurations have encoded the intrinsic patterns of spatial behaviour of users. The decoding of that information through a methodology that can quantitatively and qualitatively analyse the spatial configurations is needed.

4.2.1 Sample selection

India is a vast country with a lot of diversity. Urban cores of five developing cities in central India with similar topographic and climatic conditions are selected for the study. There are number of softwares available; and after the study and exploring the use of few softwares, Depthmap 10 by UCL is identified and used for the study (refer Section 2.7.2).

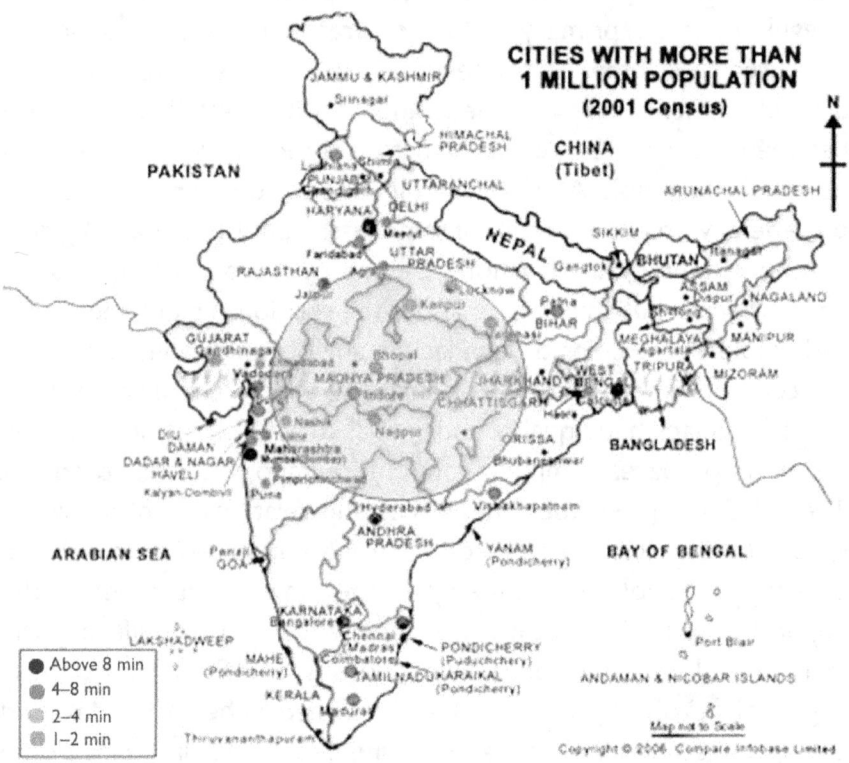

Figure 4.2 Map of India with selected cities

The criteria for selection of samples for the cities are mentioned below:

(a) Climate
(b) Developing cities
(c) Size (population)
(d) Similar urban structure (ring radial) with core of old city

(e) Cultural differences due to predominant religion (Hindu/Islamic)

The selected cities are Nagpur (Maharashtra), Bhopal (Madhya Pradesh), Varanasi (Uttar Pradesh), Lucknow (Uttar Pradesh) and Nashik (Maharashtra), whose urban cores are analyzed (Fig. 4.2). All are developing cities with population ranging within 1–2 million, as per 2001 census. The climatic conditions are tropical or subtropical climate. The elevation of these cities from mean sea level is varying between 100 and 500 m above mean sea level. Although the densities are varying in these cities but only core areas which are organically evolved are considered. These cores are mostly the dense parts of the cities. These urban cores are at the geographical centre of the present cities with ring radial pattern of road network.

4.2.2   Bhopal

Bhopal (Bhopal Municipal Corporation, 2011) is one of the historic cities whose origins are little obscure. It is said that Raja Bhoj, the famous Parmar king of Dhar, founded Bhopal City in the 11th century at its present site. The original name of the city was Bhojpal which was eventually corrupted to Bhopal. Raja Bhoj created the Upper Lake by constructing an earthen dam across the Kolans River. The traces of the original town, however, do not remain. The city was established again and fortified in the 18th century by Dost Mohammed Khan, a chieftain of Aurangzeb, when he was invited by Rani Kamalawati as a protector of her territory. The Lower Lake was created by Nawab Chhote Khan in 1794. The city remained a capital of a feudal state till it was merged in the Indian union in 1948.

Bhopal city lies in a hilly terrain, which slopes towards north and southeast. The remarkable topography of the city provides enchanting and panoramic views of the city and of its natural scenic beauty. The general ground level is between 460 and 500 m along the city. There are 14 water bodies in and around Bhopal which includes the two large lakes: upper and lower lake. The city enjoys a moderate climate. Normally temperature ranges between 10°C and 40°C, although highest temperature occasionally rises to 45°C.

The average annual rainfall is round 1200 mm, falling predominantly during July and August ('Bhopal,' 2012). After Independence, Bhopal witnessed substantial population growth due to establishment of Industrial Township by BHEL. As per 2001 census, the population of Bhopal is 1.43 million. Bhopal is an administrative state capital of Madhya Pradesh. In the core area, there are small scale industries and also number of large retail businesses. It has dominating percentage, almost 35%, of Muslim population. The location and configuration of traditional core of Bhopal is shown in Fig. 4.3.

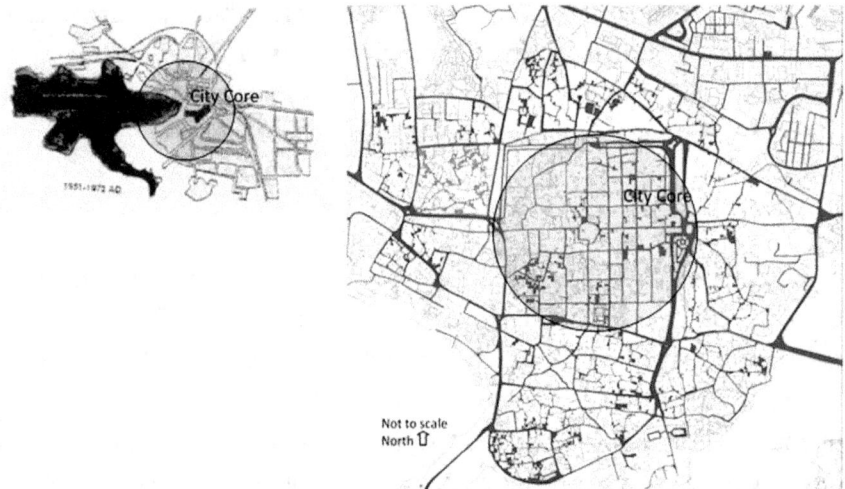

Figure 4.3 Bhopal: Core area

4.2.3 Lucknow

Lucknow is a state capital of Uttar Pradesh. As per Census 2001, the estimated population of the Lucknow is 2.18 million (Lucknow Municipal Corporation, 2006). Lucknow has traditionally been associated with *chikan* embroidery work. There are small-scale and household-based units which are located in the core area. Lucknow is also a major centre for investigation and development (R&D) and an education centre. It has Hindu population of 71% and Muslims about 26%. There are also small groups of Sikhs, Jains, Christians and Buddhists. The city has a humid subtropical climate with a cool dry winter from December to February and a hot summer from April to

June. The temperature extremes vary from about 45°C in the summer to 3°C in the winter. The city receives about 100 cm of annual rainfall mostly from the southwest monsoons between July and September. The city lies at an average altitude of 110 m above mean sea level and generally slopes to the east. While the city has archaeological remains dating back to 3000 BC, the first documented reference to Lucknow is from the 13th century when Emperor Akbar divided the Mughal Empire into twelve provinces and chose Lucknow as the seat of Government for Oudh – the most prosperous province of the empire. In the late 18th century, the Shia Nawabs of Lucknow built several imposing structures, commercial and trading centres that increased the grandeur and opulence of the city. At the time of the first war of independence in 1857, the city suffered a lot of damages and the old past was replaced with new developments during the British period. After independence, the city experienced tremendous growth and the distinct 'Lucknow' culture is slowly disappearing. There are many magnificent monuments symbolizing the glorious past of the city including the famous Imambaras ('Lucknow,' 2012). The location and configuration of traditional core of Lucknow is shown in Fig. 4.4.

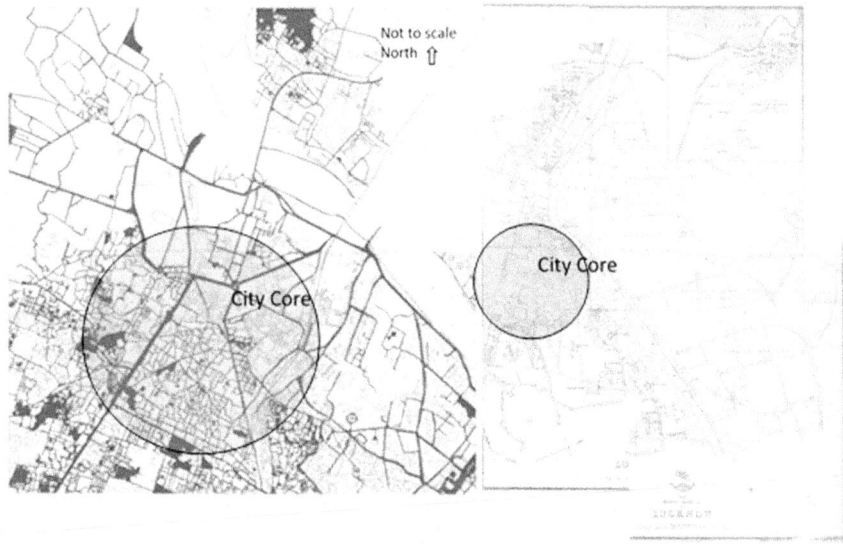

Figure 4.4 Lucknow: Core area

4.2.4 Varanasi

Varanasi (Municipal Corporation Varanasi, 2011) is one of the holiest places as far as Hinduism is concerned, and it is a religious capital of India. Varanasi is one of the oldest cities in continuous habitation in the world, with a history dating back to more than 3000 years.

It is a major religious, cultural and educational centre of India. Varanasi is also famous for its handicrafts and silk-weaving industry. The river Ganges has the world-famous ghats on the left bank. The climate of the city is of tropical nature with extreme temperature, varying from a minimum of 5°C in winter to a maximum of 45°C in summer.

The annual rainfall varies from 680 mm to 1500 mm, with a large proportion occurring during the monsoon season in the months of July to September. It is at an elevation of 80.71 m above mean sea level. The city can be divided into three distinct zones: the old city of the ghat area, the western and northern edge and the peripheral area comprising of the trans-Varuna area ('Varanasi,' 2012). The old city has a high density core area with narrow, inorganic street patterns. It has a concentration of religious structures, bazaars and old buildings with traditional architecture. The total population of the city is 1.09 million, as per 2001 census. The location and configuration of traditional core of Varanasi is shown in Fig. 4.5.

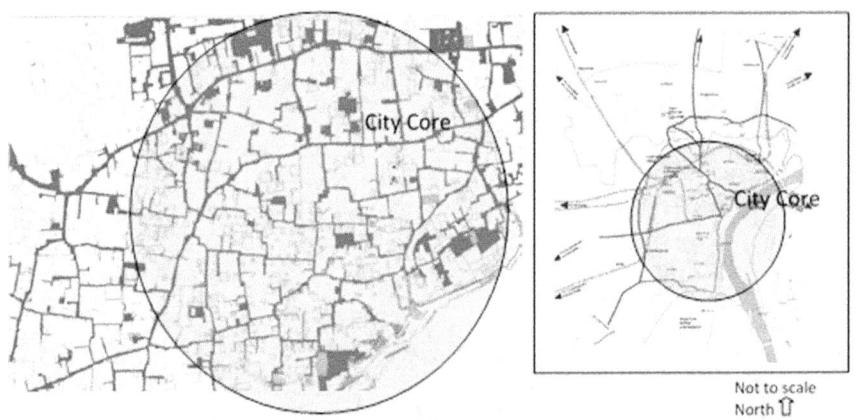

Figure 4.5 Varanasi: Core area

4.2.5 Nashik

Nashik ('Nashik,' 2012) is predominantly a holy Hindu pilgrimage city, but is now becoming a cosmopolitan town due to industrialization. Nashik has transformed from a small pilgrimage town to a modern mid-sized city in the last two decades. It is claimed to be the fastest growing city in Maharashtra. Nashik has a mild climate for most of the year apart from the hot summers which last from March to mid-June. The period from June to September is the Monsoon season, which sees about 620 mm of rain. The city experiences a mild, dry winter from November to February, with warm days and cools nights, although occasional cold waves can drop temperatures. The elevation from mean sea level is 427 m. The temperature ranges between 10°C and 37°C. According to the Census of India 2001, Nashik had a population of around 1.1 million. Nashik has been blessed with a number of small rivers besides river Godavari.

It is believed that Lord Rama resided over here during his period of exile. Due to the importance of river Godavari, the religious culture has been developed since historical era. The old city was developed during Peshwa period. Many structures, temples, bathing ghats, big residential buildings called 'Wadas' were constructed during this period ('Nashik,' 2012). The location and configuration of traditional core of Nashik is shown in Fig. 4.6.

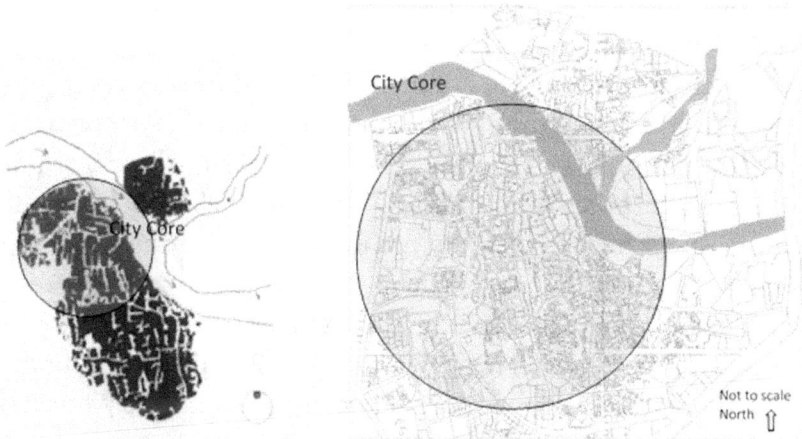

Figure 4.6 Nashik: Core area

4.2.6 Nagpur

Nagpur (Nagpur Improvement Trust, 2011) is the largest city in the central India. With a population of around 2.5 million, Nagpur is the 13th largest urban conglomeration in India.

In addition to being the seat of annual winter session of Maharashtra state assembly 'Vidhan Sabha', Nagpur is a major commercial and political centre of the Vidarbha region of Maharashtra. It is also famous throughout the country as 'Orange City' for being a major trade centre of oranges that are cultivated in the region. The city also derives political importance from being the headquarters for the Hindu nationalist organization RSS and an important location for the Dalit Buddhist movement.

Nagpur lies precisely at the centre of the country with the Zero Mile Marker indicating the geographical centre of India. The city was founded by the Gonds but later became part of the Maratha Empire under the Bhosales. The British East India Company took over Nagpur in the 19th century and made it the capital of the Central Provinces and Berar. After the first reorganization of states, the city lost its capital status but according to the informal 'Nagpur Pact' between political leaders, it was made the second capital of Maharashtra ('Nagpur,' 2012; Shah, n.d.). Nagpur is having more than 90% of the population engaged in tertiary sector (non-agricultural economic activities). It is growing as a centre for professional education. It is a cosmopolitan city with more than 25% population belonging to schedule castes and scheduled tribes. Nagpur lies on the Deccan Plateau of the Indian Peninsula and has a mean altitude of 310 m above sea level. Nagpur city is dotted with natural and manmade lakes, with Ambazari Lake being the largest. Sonegaon Lake and Gandhisagar Lake are manmade lakes created by historical rulers. Nag river, Pilli *nadi* (river) along with *nallas* (streams) form the natural drainage pattern for the city. Nagpur is known for its greenery. Nagpur has a tropical wet and dry climate with dry conditions prevailing for most of the year. Nagpur city receives an annual rainfall of 1,205 mm from monsoon rains during June to September. Summers are extremely hot lasting from March to June, with maximum temperatures occurring in May. Winter lasts from November to January, during which temperature can drop below 10°C. In 2001, the urban population of Nagpur was 2.1 million. The city contains people from other Indian states as well as people belonging to the world's major faiths, and yet is known for staying calm during communal conflicts in India. The location and configuration of traditional core of Nagpur is shown in Fig. 4.7.

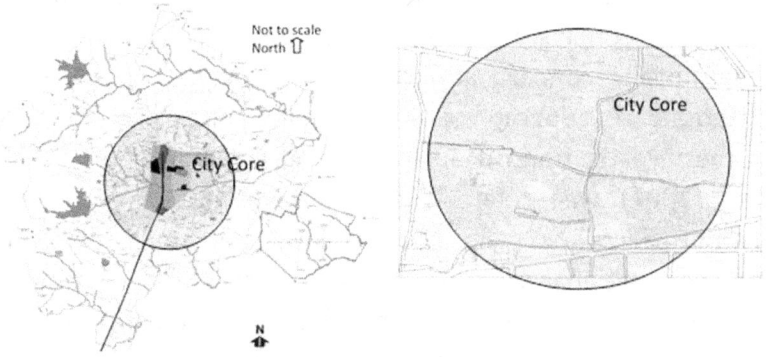

Figure 4.7 Nagpur: Core area

4.2.7 Planned built environment: Chandigarh

Traditional built environments including the analyzed traditional urban cores of select cities are multilayered. Chandigarh is one of the first totally planned and designed built environments in India. It's one of the pioneering efforts in post-independent India which has formulated an approach to deal/evolve modern built environments in India. To understand if there is any major configurational difference between this planned built environment and the organically evolved built environments, the syntactic analysis of Chandigarh was done.

4.3 Procedure

The configurations of select urban cores are investigated by representing them in terms of system of spaces through axial maps. Configuration parameters such as connectivity, local and global integration, and interpretive parameters such as intelligibility and synergy are considered. For understanding user interface with spatial configuration and reasons behind it, the placement of important urban elements, such as landmarks in the overall spatial configuration, are observed.

Annexure II gives details of syntactic analysis of select urban cores. The deduced syntactic identity in Indian built environments was then reviewed with respect to other parts of the world, referring the already conducted investigation works through secondary sources. The concerns about the validity of space syntax methodology in Indian context and subjectivity in interpretation of analytical conclusions can only be resolved by conducting the study. Another concern about syntactic analysis is: whether the implications of topography are reflected in the analysis or not. For that, the investigation on 'axial lines and contour lines' by Valerio Cutini (2007) was referred. It was investigated if altimetrical variations affect the configurational indices of the built environment, when syntactic analysis is done; using space syntax methodology, it was found that the orographic features get reflected in the system of spaces and thus gets reflected indirectly in the syntactic analysis as well (Valerio, 2007). Thus, after ensuring the validity of the methodology to be used for the analysis, syntactic analysis of the select urban cores is done.

4.4 Analysis

The global integration map of Nagpur is shown in Fig. 4.8. It can be seen that the overall system of spaces forms a sort of orthogonal grid at the global level as it connects as well as segregates the area with rest of the urban system. The same orthogonal grid is not continued in the residential clusters. The subsystems formed within the system have truly organic pattern with tree system of spaces. The analysis through queries has highlighted that these are the areas with higher mean depth and low connectivity. This makes these areas less integrated, less intelligible and permeable, thus avoiding unnecessary through traffic. Slightly segregated spaces from the global grid are conducive for outdoor activities, social interactions and are also used as play areas. Every subsystem has a sort of peripheral road which gives immediate access to internal residential areas to join the global movement which is mostly vehicular. Yet internal organic and tree pattern of system encourages pedestrian movement.

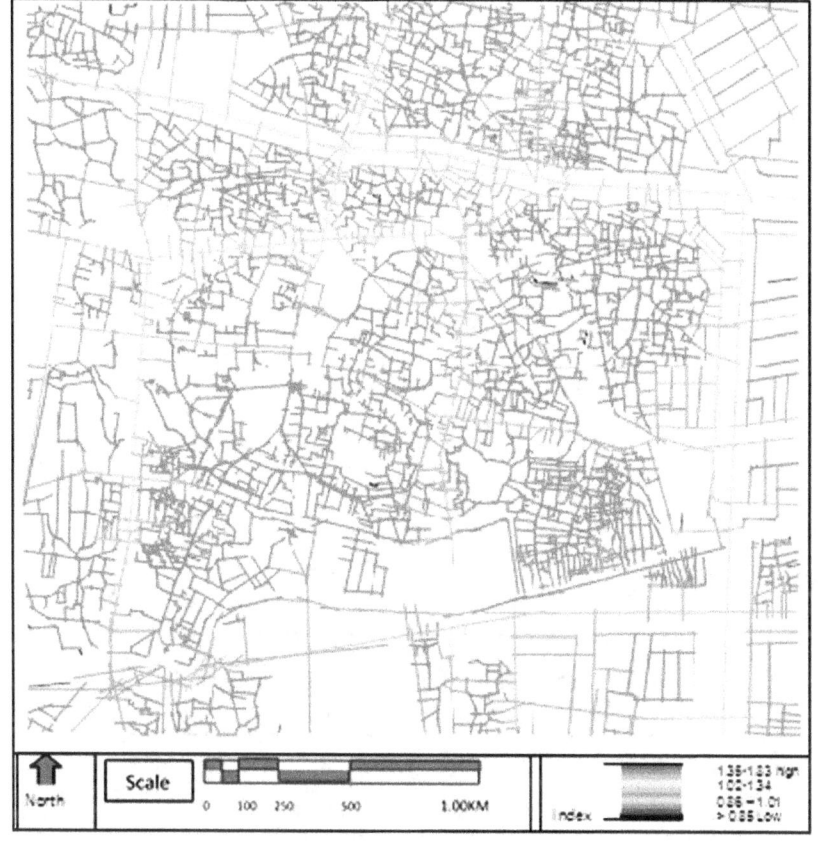

Figure 4.8 Integration (Rn) map of urban core (Mahal) of Nagpur

The global integration map of Bhopal is shown in Fig. 4.9. For Bhopal, there is a system of spaces with orthogonal grid in walled city area, making it quite intelligible for users. It was a walled city, and entry of the outsiders or strangers was totally restricted. However, the same orthogonal grid is not continued in the area surrounding the walled city. The subsystems formed outside the walled area are truly organic with tree system of spaces. The query result has highlighted that these are the areas with higher than average mean depth (2.5) and lower than average connectivity (2.5). This makes these areas less intelligible and totally impermeable thus protecting the central walled area. Highly segregated subsystems are without coherent global system. The water bodies have further segregated the urban system from the extended system.

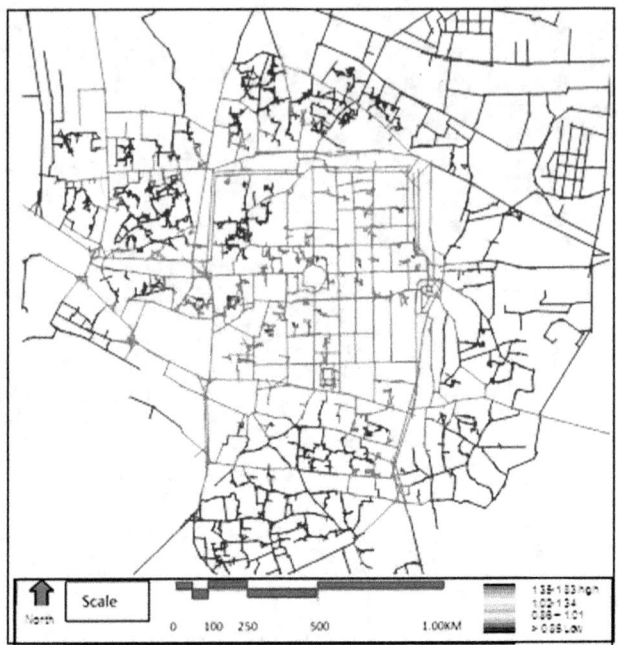

Figure 4.9 Integration (Rn) map of urban core of Bhopal

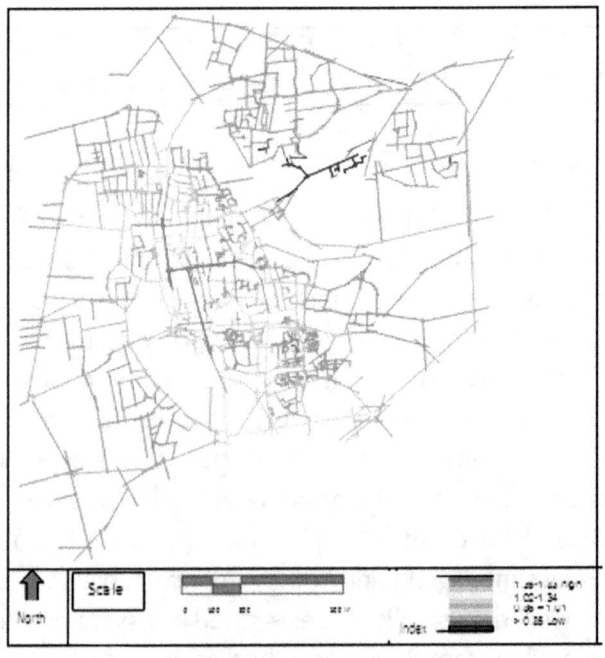

Figure 4.10 Integration (Rn) map of urban core of Nashik

The global integration map of Nashik is shown in Fig. 4.10. In Nashik, there is a system of spaces with deformed orthogonal grid in central area with high integration and connectivity, making it quite intelligible for users. Though it is on the banks of river Godavari, the system of spaces is not orientated to the river. The subsystem formed outside is radial separated from central area by a ring road. The part of old area on the other bank is quite segregated due to the river in between.

Figure 4.11 shows global integration map of Varanasi. There is a system of spaces with deformed radial grid oriented towards the holy river Ganges. The local u parts are quite segregated, and every part is finally oriented towards the river 'Ganges'. The visual and physical linkages to the river are established. However, the radial grid forming the global system is not continued in the local areas. The local areas are less intelligible and totally impermeable. This may be an effort to protect the city from number of Islamic invasions from time to time 10th century onwards. The access to water is easily possible for locals, yet the global system is highly unintelligible, making the city impermeable and inaccessible to strangers from riverside.

Figure 4.11 Integration (Rn) map of urban core of Lucknow

The global integration map of Lucknow is shown in Fig. 4.12. The overall system of spaces is radiating from the political and religious core on the banks of river Gomati. The local subsystems are not oriented towards the river, unlike Varanasi. The same radial grid is not continued in the residential clusters. The subsystems formed within the system are truly organic with tree pattern. This makes these areas less intelligible and permeable, thus avoiding unnecessary through traffic. Slightly segregated spaces from the global grid, yet having better integration at local level, are present inside residential clusters. There is very poor synergy between parts and whole. Part of the old city on other bank is quite segregated.

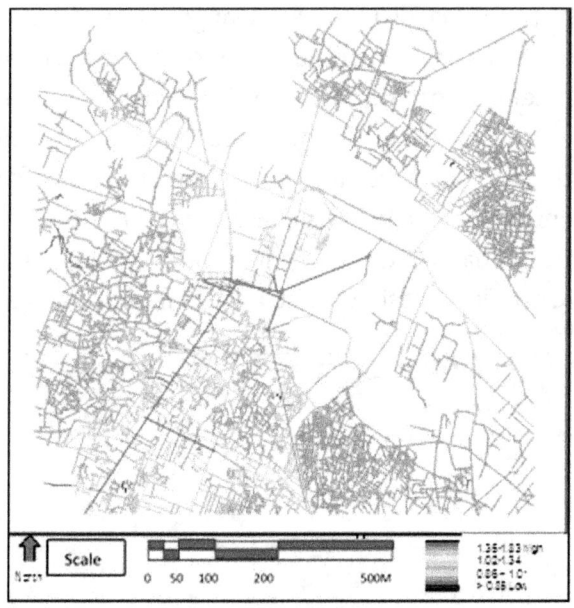

Figure 4.12 Integration (Rn) map of urban core of Varanasi

In case of Chandigarh, there are lesser but longer axes compared to any of the traditional urban cores. Figure 4.13 shows global integration map of Chandigarh. Mean depth is also very low. Thus many spaces have very high local and global integration. The connectivity of each axis is also very high. The syntactic analysis of Chandigarh has shown that though planned in grid iron pattern, it is not much intelligible. Neighbourhood planning has imparted it a well-deserved synergy (Fig. 4.13).

Figure 4.13 Integration (Rn) map of Chandigarh

4.5 Numerical synthesis

Numerical synthesis of syntactic parameters of traditional urban cores is done to find out if there is any syntactic identity. It is compared with syntactic parameters of Chandigarh.

Table 4.1 Number of axes

Cities	Area in sq km	Number of Axes	Correlation Coefficient	Remarks
Bhopal	3.2	2686	0.24	Significant positive correlation for Bhopal, Nashik and Nagpur and not for Lucknow and Varanasi
Nashik	2.5	1232	1.00	
Nagpur	4.1	4360		
Lucknow	2.6	4502		No. of axes are much more than area in case of Lucknow and Varanasi, making these cities fragmented and unintelligible, impermeable
Varanasi	2.8	5654		

There is a significant positive relationship between number of axes and square kilometre area in case of urban cores of Nagpur, Nashik and Bhopal (Table 4.1; Fig. 4.14). However, the number of axes is much higher, irrespective of area in case of Varanasi and Lucknow. The number of axes is highest in case of Varanasi, making it the most fragmented city followed by Lucknow.

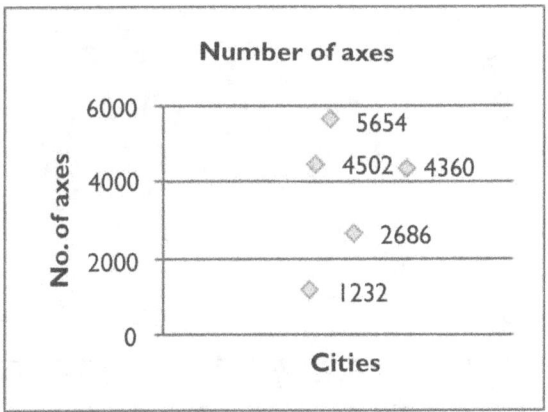

Figure 4.14 Relationship between number of axes and area

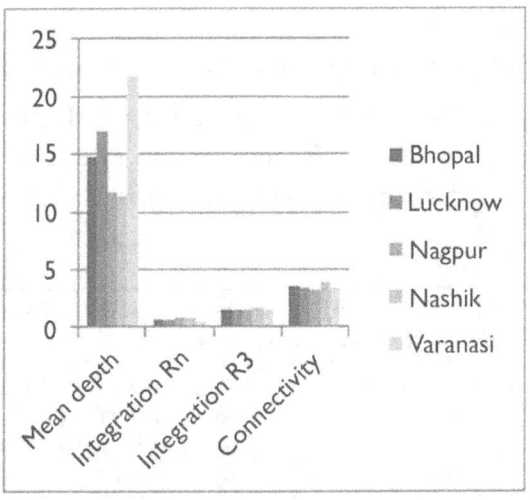

Figure 4.15 Synergy and intelligibility of Chandigarh in comparison to traditional Indian urban cores

The comparative analysis of syntactic parameters of select urban cores of central Indian cities tends to show similar syntactic properties with some variations (Fig. 4.15). When compared with chandigarh, there are some diffferences. Intelligibility and synergy are highest for Chandigarh followed by the urban core of Nagpur, then Nashik and Bhopal. Lucknow and Varanasi are equally poor in terms of synergy and intelligibility.

Though the urban cores of select Indian cities show similar syntactic identity, there are pairs of cities, Bhopal–Lucknow, Nagpur–Nashik, which show distinctions from other pairs. Nagpur and Nashik have similar syntactic identity as they both are cosmopolitan cities with major percentage of population belonging to Hindu religion. The syntactic parameters are similar for Bhopal and Lucknow. The two cities have similar social environment as the substantial percentage of population belongs to Muslim community. The core areas are dominated by Muslim population in both the cities. Hence in table, these cities are highlighted with same colour.

Varanasi is the oldest Hindu pilgrimage centre, and the syntactic parameters are quite different than other four cores. This is because of the social environment and the typical geographical setting as well. The importance given to the river Ganges for most of the religious rituals has also resulted into the typical spatial configuration. The syntactic parameters of core of Ahmedabad are referred from investigation by Shibu Raman. The syntactic parameters of Ahmedabad are almost comparable to the values of traditional cores of select five cities. This established that there is a syntactic identity for Indian cities which can be described in terms of average values given in Table 4.2.

The traditional settlements have lot of variations in terms of integration values. This makes interior spaces with high depth and thus very less physically integrated, making them conducive for high social integrations. The peripheral spaces are with high physical integration. This variation and modulation from high depth to low depth and subsequently high integration to low integration is somehow lost in modern built environments planned on the modern principles of planning, experimented with Chandigarh (Figs. 4.13 and 4.16). These are not in accordance with the user preferences in terms of space proxemics in Indian context. These principles of planning are different than the principles of urbanism, specific to Indian context. It has

Table 4.2 Syntactic parameters: Traditional cities and Chandigarh

Name of the cities	Mean depth			Integration Rn			Integration R3			Connectivity			Intelligibility	Synergy
	Min	Ave.	Max	Min	Ave.	Max	Min	Ave	Max	Min	Ave	Max		
Bhopal	1	14.82	27.73	0.21	0.64	5.09	0.21	1.53	5.09	0	3.5	22	0.065	0.25
Lucknow	1	16.89	31.38	0.21	0.61	1.08	0.21	1.53	4.19	0	3.3	48	0.029	0.17
Nagpur	1	11.62	20.2	0.21	0.9	1.83	0.21	1.59	3.97	0	3.27	33	0.17	0.51
Nashik	12.4	11.36	27.15	0.29	0.76	1.27	0.33	1.68	3.37	0	3.82	21	0.12	0.33
Varanasi	1	21.73	40.75	0.21	0.49	5.09	0.21	1.5	5.09	0	3.42	35	0.026	0.15
Average		15.284			0.68			1.566			3.46		0.082	0.282
Ahmedabad					0.8			1.74			2.97		0.115	0.193
Chandigarh	1	6.48	19.97	0.21	1.62	3.04	0.21	2.14	4.78	0	3.77	66	0.13	0.82

lot of social implications as well. There are obviously many positive aspects about planning and design of Chandigarh. This analysis is not to disregard one of the most important planning endeavor in India and its positive impacts later on developments. The point is to understand the configurational difference with respect to traditional Indian built environments.

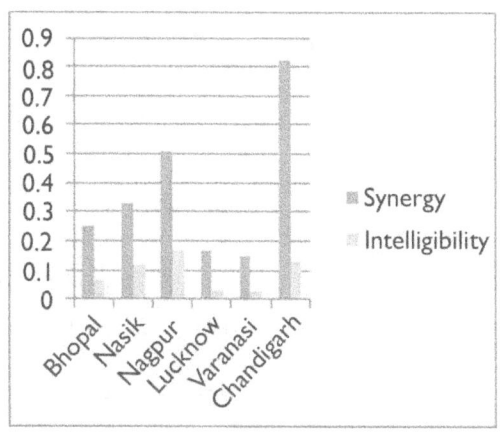

Figure 4.16 Traditional urban cores: Syntactic parameters

4.5.1 Syntactic parameters – world scenario

Syntactic parameters of traditional Indian built environments are compared with built environments from other parts of the world. These are referred from secondary sources (Fig. 4.17).

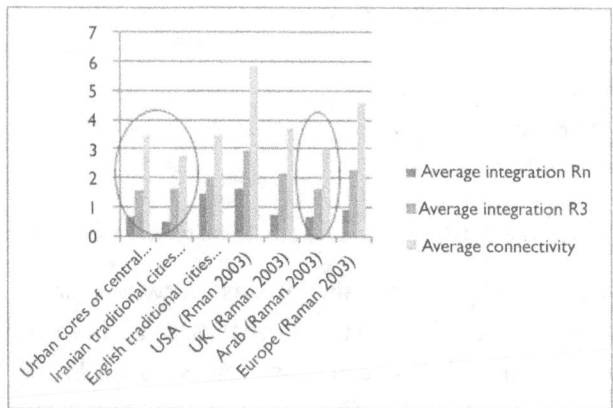

Figure 4.17 Syntactic parameters: Indian and other built environments

Table 4.3 Syntactic parameters: World scenario

Name of the cities	Number of cases	Average integration Rn	Average integration R3	Average connectivity	Average intelligibility	Average synergy
Urban cores of central Indian cities	5	0.68	1.566	3.46	0.082	0.282
Iranian traditional cities (Karimi, 1997)	6	0.482	1.6	2.772	0.116	0.16
English traditional cities (Karimi and Kayvan, 1997)	6	1.44	2.02	3.45	0.264	0.427
USA (Raman, 2003)	12	1.61	2.956	5.835	0.224	0.559
UK (Raman, 2003)	13	0.72	2.148	3.713	0.124	0.232
Arab (Raman, 2003)	18	0.65	1.619	2.975	0.231	0.16
Europe (Raman, 2003)	15	0.918	2.254	4.609	0.224	0.559

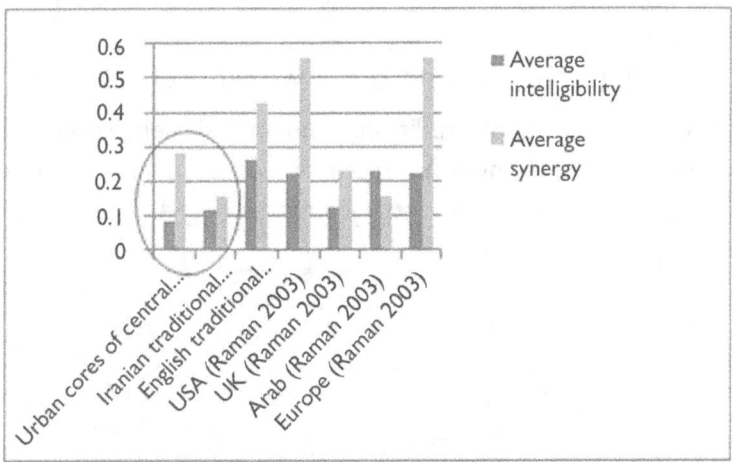

Figure 4.18 Synergy and intelligibility: Comparison

There are configuration similarities between urban cores of central Indian cities and Iranian traditional cities and Arab cities. These cities also have organic pattern of spatial system. The intelligibility of urban cores of central Indian cities is low but they are better synergistic compared to Iranian or Arab cities (Fig. 4.18).

4.6 Traditional settlements – configurational peculiarities

The syntactic analysis of the traditional Indian settlements has tried to establish the problems associated in studying organically evolved built environments of urban cores in central Indian cities. It has helped in better understanding the built environments in terms of its structure/configuration. Organically evolved settlements appear chaotic but they are not 'disorderly'. The analysis proved that though the organic settlement, which apparently seems to be lacking any structure, does have structure; and it is evolved w.r.t. user preferences about space proxemics. These traditional built environments appear humane as there is congruence between user preferences in terms of space proxemics and the configuration of the built environment.

As far as the select traditional built environments are studied, there is a syntactic identity. It is different from the configuration of planned city, Chandigarh. The traditionally evolved urban built environments have poor intelligibility yet comparatively higher local integrations and better synergy, making local spaces more socially cohesive, and hence humane. In case of traditional built environments, variations in physical integration amongst the spaces help to maintain the social integration. Highly segregated interior residential streets become socially integrated at the local level as they are separated from public and vehicular domain. Highly integrated spaces emerge as social spaces at the global or city level. These variations help to maintain the required hierarchy between the spaces of the built environment, which is not getting emulated appropriately in contemporary built environments.

The notion of spatial segregation, rationality and intelligibility associated with post-industrial revolution urban planning norms is quite different and at times irrelevant in Indian built environments. It is not necessary to emulate the traditional configurations evolved in historic times. To contribute positively to the evolution of contemporary Indian built environments, one can use the configuration understanding with reasons.

4.7 References

- Bhopal (2012). In *Wikipedia, the Free Encyclopedia*. Retrieved from http://en.wikipedia.org/w/index.php?title=Bhopal&oldid=514364611

- Bhopal Municipal Corporation (2011). *Bhopal City Development Plan under JNNURM*. Bhopal. Retrieved May 19, 2011 from http://www.indiaenvironmentportal.org.in/files/Bhopal%20CDP_Final%20.pdf
- Census of India: Provisional Population Totals India: Paper 1: Census 2011. Retrieved September 9, 2011, from http://www.censusindia.gov.in/2011-prov-results/prov_results_paper1_india.html
- Kader, A. I. (2010). *Natural Elements Determining the Urban Form, Case: River Godavary. City Nasik*. Master's Thesis at CEPT, Ahmadabad.
- Karimi, K. (1997). *The Spatial Logic of Organic Cities in Iran and the United Kingdome*. In *Proceedings Volume I*. Presented at the Space Syntax First International Symposium, London. Retrieved from http://www.spacesyntax.net/symposia-archive/SSS1
- Lucknow (2012). In *Wikipedia, the Free Encyclopedia*. Retrieved from http://en.wikipedia.org/w/index.php?title=Lucknow&oldid=514089880
- Lucknow Municipal Corporation (2006). *City development plan, Lucknow*. Lucknow. Retrieved January 23, 2011, from http://lmc.up.nic.in/nnfinal.pdf
- Municipal Corporation Varanasi (2011). *City Development Plan for Varanasi*. Varanasi. Retrieved May 18, 2011 from http://jnnurm.nic.in/cdp-of-varanasi.html
- Nagpur (2012). In *Wikipedia, the Free Encyclopedia*. Retrieved from http://en.wikipedia.org/w/index.php?title=Nagpur&oldid=514486048
- Nagpur Improvement Trust (2011). *City Development Plan, Nagpur*. Nagpur. Retrieved from April 22, 2011 http://www.nitnagpur.org/dp.html#masterplan
- Nasik (2012). In *Wikipedia, the Free Encyclopedia*. Retrieved from http://en.wikipedia.org/w/index.php?title=Nashik&oldid=514334988
- Nasik Municipal Corporation (2006). *City Development Plan, Nasik*. Nasik. Retrieved March 17, 2011 from http://nashikcorporation.gov.in/pagedetail.aspx?id=22&mid=70
- Raman, S. (2003). *Communities and Spatial Culture in a Communally Diverse City: Ahmadabad, India*. In 4th International Space Syntax Symposium, London, University College. Retrieved March 24, 2010 from http://www.spacesyntax.net/symposia-archive/SSS4/fullpapers/74Ramanpaper.pdf
- Shah, D. (n.d.). Manifestations for a City [HONOURABLE MENTION] | Resilient City. Retrieved November 10, 2012, from http://www.resilientcity.org/index.cfm?PAGEPATH=Competition/Manifestations_for_a_City__HONOURABLE_MENTION_&ID=23091
- Valerio, C. (2007). *Axial Lines and Contour Lines*. In Proceedings of 6th International Space Syntax Symposium. Presented at the Sixth International Space Syntax Symposium, Istanbul, Turkey. Retrieved May 20, 2010 from www.spacesyntaxistanbul.itu.edu.tr/papers
- Varanasi (2012). In *Wikipedia, the Free Encyclopedia*. Retrieved from http://en.wikipedia.org/w/index.php?title=Varanasi&oldid=514360517

Chapter 5

Photo: Ganshesh Festival, West High Court Road, Nagpur

Chapter 5

User preferences in contemporary cities

Abstract: In the last chapter, we have discussed user preferences in traditional settlements. Here, the influence of configurations on development of user preferences or cognitive constructs in contemporary cities is studied in case of Nagpur. It is taken as a representative example of developing cities in India. This chapter discusses the study to understand the relationship between spatial cognition and configuration other way, i.e. cognition as dependent of configuration. The syntactic analysis of the whole city and two select localities with different configurations is done. Cognitive constructs of users are assessed through primary surveys. Analytical conclusions inferred about user preferences.

Key words: Anthropological aspect of cognition, psychological aspect of cognition, index of use, index of recognition, user preferences

5.1 Nagpur: Evolution

Nagpur is one of the developing cities of India, which is located at the geographical centre of India. The Gonds from 1550 AD to 1748 AD ruled the city of Nagpur. Then Bhosales ruled it from 1748 AD to 1853 AD, till British took over. During Gond period, roads were constructed and the city was divided into wards. Further, a strong 3 miles long protection wall was also constructed. During the period of Bhosales, King Raghuji established two military settlements with a royal residential development 'Mahal'. Till date, this old part of the city is known as 'Mahal'. The battle of Sitaburdi was fought between Appasaheb Bhonsala and the British. A new state central province was formed with Nagpur as capital; and the city was divided into the eastern (old city) and the western part by creating a mound and laying railway line. In 1915, Sir Pattrick Geddes visited the city to propose conservative surgery for decaying medieval urban fabric. Post-independence Nagpur remained capital of Madhya Pradesh till the states were recognized on linguistic basis.

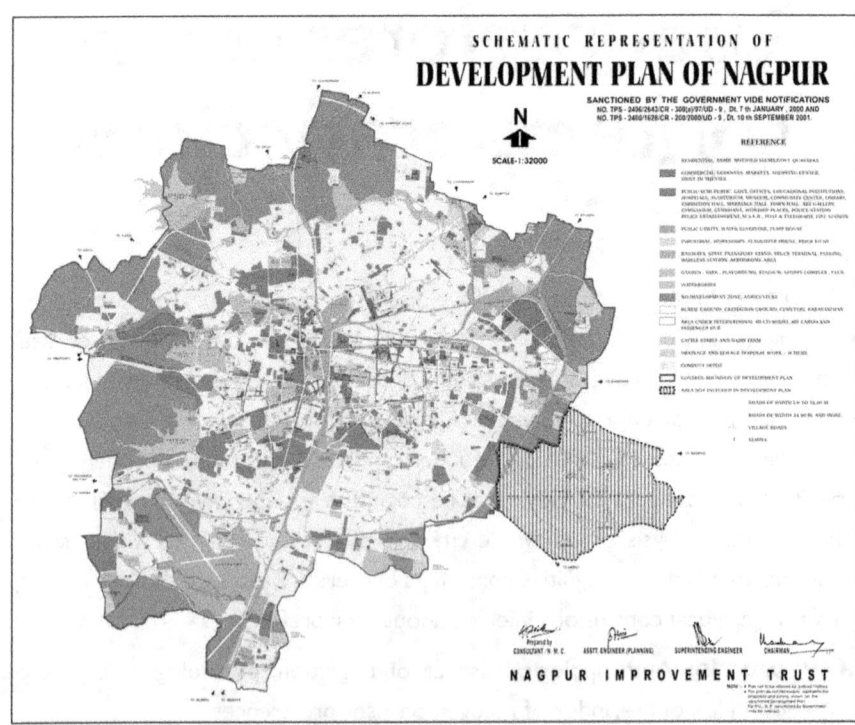

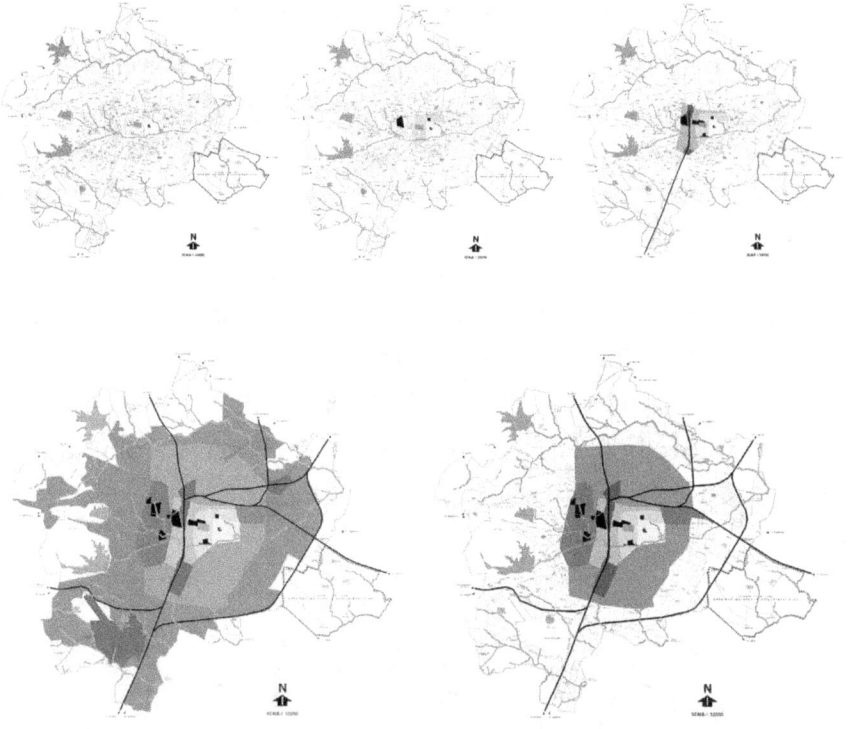

Figure 5.1 Nagpur: Settlement evolution

There is a significant growth and rise in urban population of Nagpur in the last 50 years. As per 2001 census, the urban population of Nagpur was 2.1 million. The population in 1865 was about 0.025 million, which have increased to about 2.5 million in 150 years history of Nagpur Municipal Corporation. Today, Nagpur is the second capital of Maharashtra and continues to grow in terms of an administrative, educational and cultural centre in the Vidarbha region. Nagpur as an industrial city is yet to develop; though it has been chosen for development of international special economic zone (SEZ). Due to its locational peculiarity, the Multimodal International Hub Airport (MIHAN) is under development at Nagpur. Because of the developed infrastructure and its centralized location, instead of heavy industries, IT industry has shown remarkable progress in the recent past.

5.2 Syntactic analysis of Nagpur

To find out the syntactic parameters of the whole city to understand its configuration, syntactic analysis of Nagpur city was done. The syntactic parameters of the city and the traditional core are compared. The change in land-use pattern or emergence of informal sector is considered as an indicator of spatial cognition in terms of imposed order by users. The mismatch between user preferences and planning leads to conflicts / non-confirming uses / informal sector. This has also helped in identification of two localities to do study of cognition as dependent of configuration.

The updated physical map of Nagpur is collected from Nagpur Municipal Corporation (Fig. 5.2).

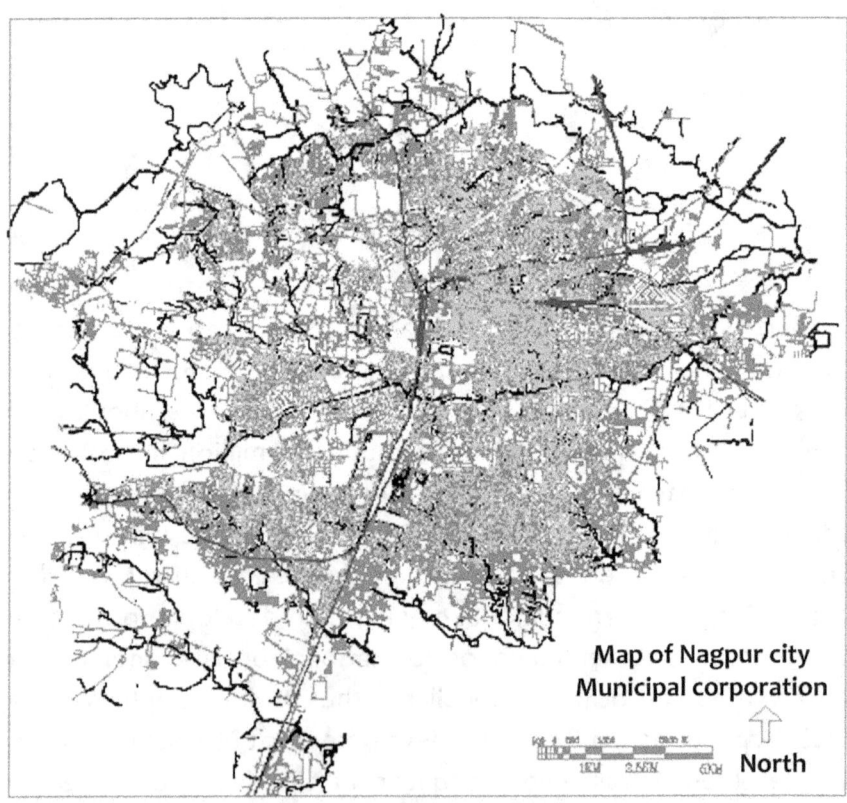

Figure 5.2 Map of Nagpur

The axial line map is derived and then syntactic analysis of the whole city is done. There is a peculiarity in the spatial configuration of the city due to railway line. North–south-oriented railway line divided the city into two distinct eastern and western parts. The east Nagpur is the old Nagpur. During British colonial period, after the induction of railway line, development started on western side of old Nagpur. It continued after independence. In general, Nagpur is spreading horizontally with ring radial pattern. The link between east and west Nagpur is very limited through three underpasses, two over bridges and two railway crossings. The syntactic analysis of the urban core of Nagpur is already discussed in Chapter 4. Amongst the select five traditional urban cores, Nagpur is having the highest values of synergy and intelligibility. Also the overall configuration shows an interesting variation in integration values. The syntactic parameters are given in Table 5.1.

Table 5.1 Syntactic parameters of Nagpur

Parameters	Min	Average	Max	Traditional core Mahal (Average values)	Remarks
No. of Axes	39713 (189.10 per sq km)			4360 (1063.41 per sq km)	Highly horizontal spread
Length of axes	0.030	90.77	4257	47.93	
Mean depth	1.66	23.85	56.2	11.62	Depth is preferred but too much of depth makes built environment fragmented
Integration Rn	0.21	0.55	6.89	0.9	Low integration
Integration R3	0.21	1.58	6.89	1.59	Average local integration is similar to core
Connectivity	0	3.13	54	3.27	Connectivity is similar
Synergy	0.10			0.51	Very low synergy
Intelligibility	0.026			0.17	Very low intelligibility though newly developed areas are in grid iron pattern

The scatter grams for synergy and intelligibility for traditional core and whole city of Nagpur are shown in Figs. 5.3 and 5.4. The comparison of syntactic analysis of the whole city and the traditional core has highlighted few aspects. Obviously bigger the area, it will become less intelligible and synergistic. Yet here the values for Nagpur have very low synergy and intelligibility, compared to the core areas. It is evolving in a fragmented manner. The number of axes is very less and the length of axes is more in newer areas compared to the core. The syntactic analysis of Nagpur is done to identify two localities to conduct primary survey for second part of the investigation.

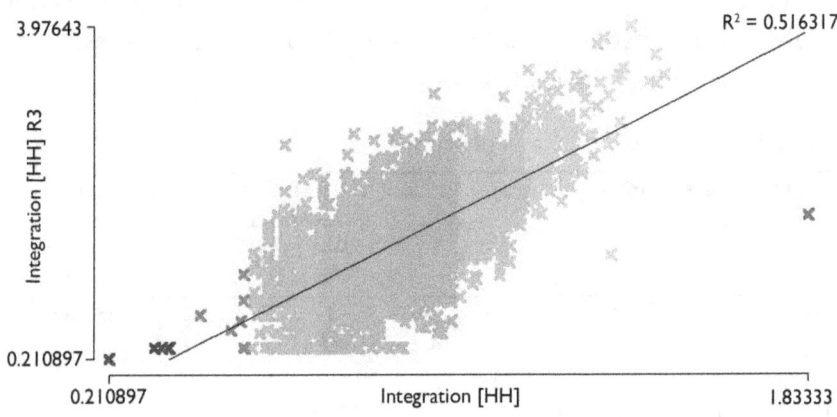

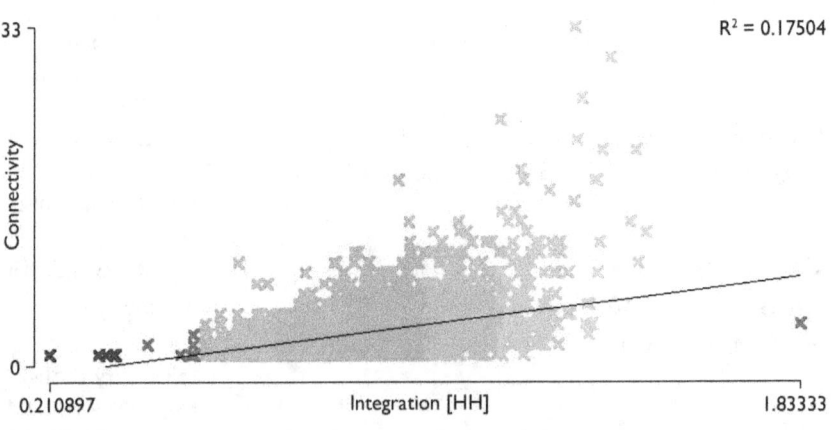

Figure 5.3 Scattergrams: Intelligibility and synergy of Nagpur

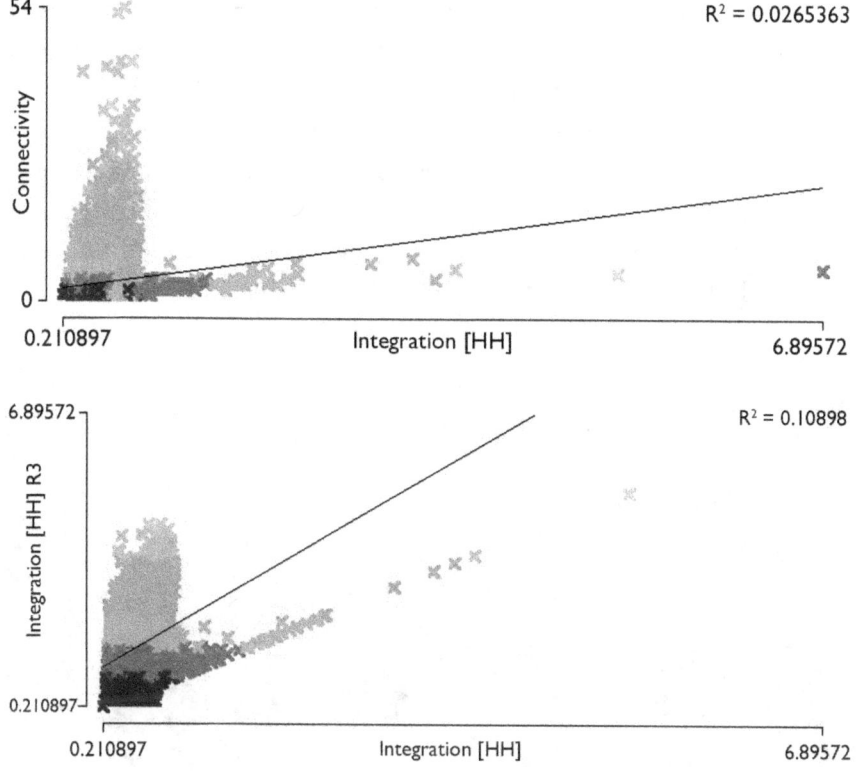

Figure 5.4 Scattergrams: Intelligibility and synergy of traditional core of Nagpur

5.2.1 Nagpur: Configurational peculiarities and user behaviours

For understanding configurational peculiarities and its implications on users' behaviour, the query application was used. The query results have highlighted:

1. The query result about streets with highest global integration values is shown in Fig. 5.5. Integration, that is accessibility, has significant role in emergence of land uses. The roads with highest values of integration have emerged as important wholesale markets at the city level. The result of query about other areas with global integration value more than 0.75 is shown in Fig. 5.6. It has shown the areas like Dhantoli where there has been tremendous rise of commercial activities,

especially the hospitals in recent past. Proposed land-use plan of these areas is shown in Fig. 5.7. Comparing it with the observed pattern of land uses, it can be inferred that areas with high global integration such as Sitabuldi have already changed land use completely from residential to commercial. On Palm Road, land use is rapidly changing from residential/ institutional to commercial. Medical square, Indora square, Umred road and Nandanwan areas are fast developing as important activity nodes at city level (Fig. 5.6).

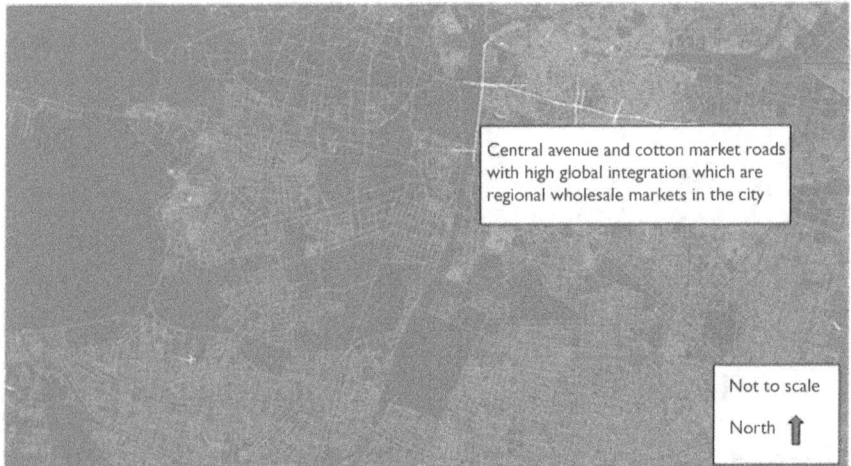

Figure 5.5 Query result of value 'Integration (HH)'>0.85

Figure 5.6 Query result of value 'Integration (HH)'>0.75

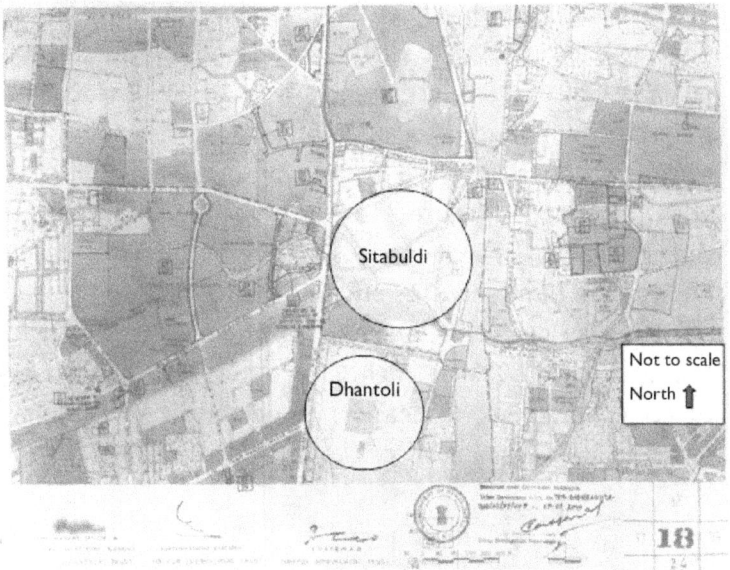

Figure 5.7 Proposed land-use plan of Dhantoli and Sitabuldi

As shown in Fig. 5.8, the radial roads like Amravati road, Wardha road, Umred road and some parts of Ring road are the roads with higher values of local integration. These areas have shown drastic changes in land uses in the last decade. They have emerged as important activity nodes at the zonal levels. The proposed land use of these roads is residential, but if observed today there are multiple commercial/institutional activities that are flourishing on these roads, making them as important social spaces.

Figure 5.8 Result of query: Value 'Integration (HH) R3' > 3.5

2. Similarly, areas with higher local integration such as Khamala Square, Hill road, West High Court road in west Nagpur and Jagnade Square, Sakkardara, Nara road in East Nagpur are emerging as important local activity nodes. Many commercial and institutional activities are located on these roads. If compared with proposed land-use plan in 2001 (Fig. 5.9), one can find that there are many changes and lot of commercialisation, emergence of mixed uses and informal sector in these activity nodes. They are also emerging as important social gathering nodes. In case of West High Court road, one can observe lot of congregations on occasion of celebrations like New Year, Christmas or winning of 'cricket world cup' (Fig. 5.10).

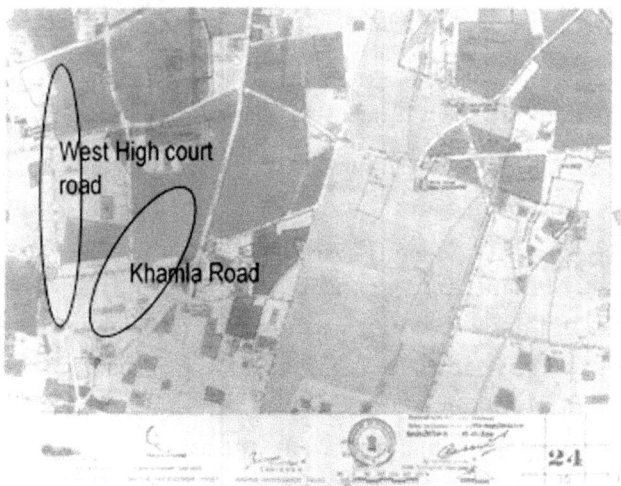

Figure 5.9 Proposed land-use plan of West Nagpur

Figure 5.10 Festive celebrations on West High Court Road

Thus, based on the syntactic analysis of Nagpur, it is clear that configuration plays an important role in development of cognition in terms of imposing order by users. The mismatch between proposed and emerging pattern of land uses show that due to configurational peculiarity, there are transformations of built environments and emergence of some important activity nodes and social spaces. Thus, it shows the role of configuration in developing spatial cognition in terms of anthropological aspect, i.e. imposing order.

3. Configurational peculiarity plays an important role in using open spaces/ streets for specific activities. It's not just configuration responsible for it but configuration seems to have affected the use of spaces significantly. Proliferation of certain informal activities takes place on streets with peculiar configurations. Availability of formal spaces hardly has any role in development of informal activities. *Chor bazar* near Empress mall is one such example. In Fig. 5.11, one can see the informal market of home appliances at the entry gate of mall which has formal shop for similar appliances. Also the configurational peculiarity is seen in the same figure. *Chor bazar* is on second order locally integrated street which connects two highly integrated streets.

Figure 5.11 Chor Bazar and its configurational peculiarity

Unavailability of proper defined open space for social, community activities is one of the reasons for use of streets as social spaces. However, it is not always the case. Even when the defined open space is available nearby, street is preferred for social and community gatherings. Figure 5.12 shows locations of community festival celebrations on street, in spite of availability of defined open space in vicinity. As seen in local integration maps of same locations shown in Fig. 5.13, it can be observed that location of *mandaps* (vernacular name for the temporary structures erected for community festivals) for installation of Ganpati, Durga idols are on second level integrated streets which have direct visual and physical link to streets with high local integration (R3).

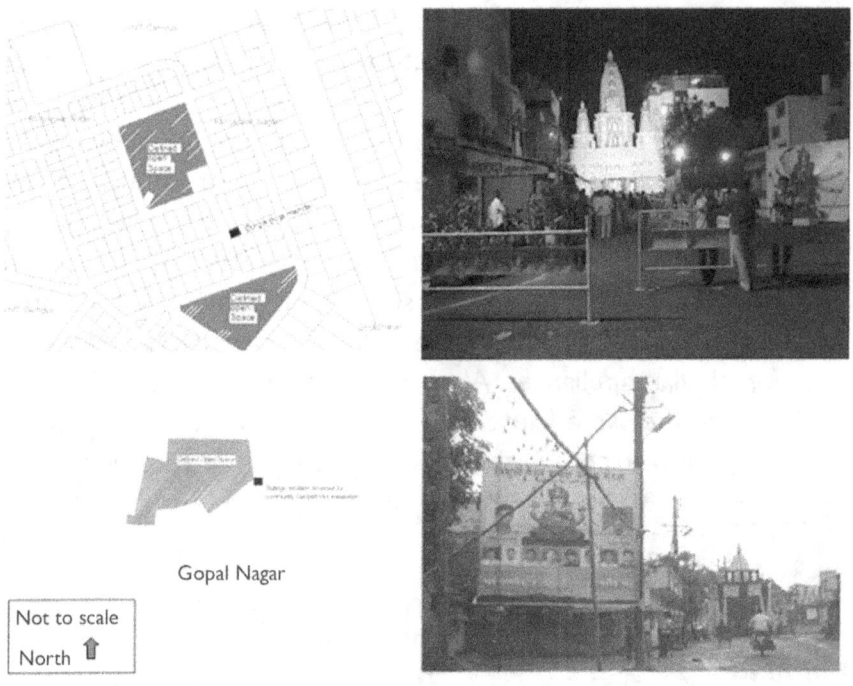

Figures 5.12 Location of installation of community Ganpati/ Durga idol: Gopal Nagar and Madhav Nagar

All sorts of activities, ranging from political rally to commercial, marketing, advertisements, recreation, religious processions, public performances, eating, etc., happen on streets which make use of streets as vibrant social space. The use of street as social space is irrespective of cast, religion or economic status of its users. Hindus use it for community festivals such as *Durga pooja, Ganesh festival*. For Buddhist festival like *Dhammachakra pravartan din,* streets are used for charity activities like free food distribution (bhojandan), free health check-up camps, public performances and marketing. In case of Id-i-milad, streets of Mominpura become live with social gatherings, festive shopping and hoardings. In low-income areas or slums, obviously activities spill over on streets due to crunch of space; but even in plush localities like Dhantoli, Ramdaspeth, or Civil Lines, streets are often used for religious and commercial activities. The use of street for social and community activities is there for inner residential areas to arterial streets or even highways. Obviously, the types of activities vary according to hierarchy of streets. Configuration certainly plays an important role in the emergence or proliferation of certain types of activities on streets.

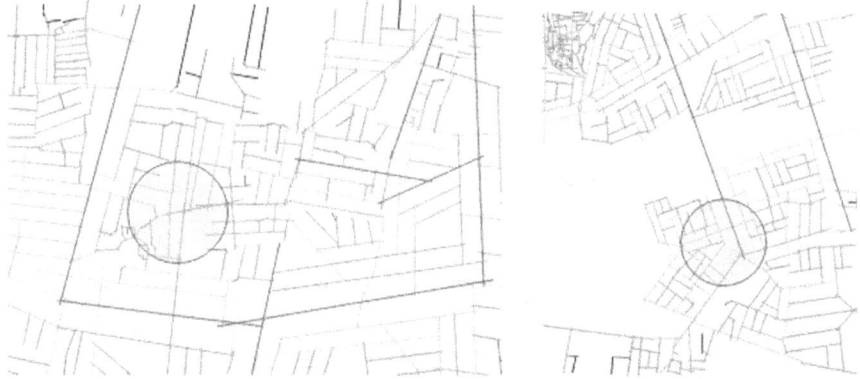

Figures 5.13 Local integration maps: Gopal and Madhav Nagar

5.3   Select localities: Syntactic properties

For area-level analysis, two localities are to be selected where primary data about spatial cognition are to be collected. One selected area is part of organically evolved traditional built environment, i.e. old Nagpur (Fig. 5.1). Second area is selected as part of planned development (west Nagpur) which is developed at least 20 years ago. Residential areas developed in post-independence period, Ravi Nagar, Dhantoli, Trimurti Nagar are short listed due to some syntactic similarity and similarity in socio-demographic characteristics. The syntactic analysis of the localities was done. Table 5.2 shows the results. Based on the analysis, 'Mahal' as a representative of old area and Trimurti Nagar as a representative of new planned area are chosen for the intended area level study (Fig. 5.14).

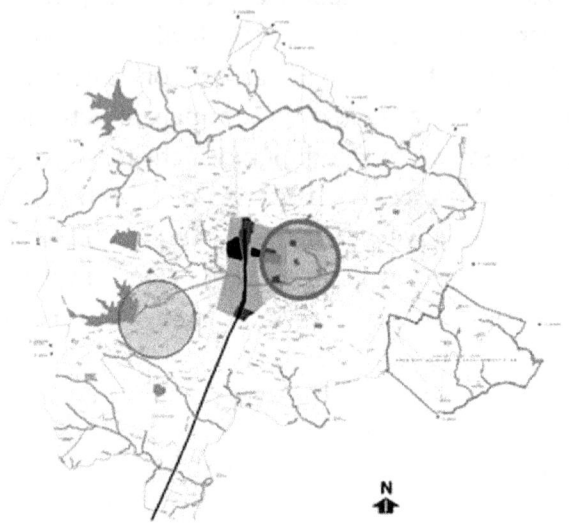

Figure 5.14 Selected localities

Table 5.2 Syntactic analysis of identified localities

Name of the areas	Mean depth			Connec-tivity		Integration Rn			Integration R3			Syn-ergy	Intelli-gibility
	Min	Ave	Max	Ave	Max	Min	Ave	Max	Min	Ave	Max		
Mahal	1	1.62	20.2	3.27	33	0.21	0.9	1.83	0.21	1.59	3.97	0.51	0.17
Dhantoli	1	10.53	19.22	3.11	19	0.35	0.7	1.81	0.33	1.5	3.24	0.33	0.14
Trimurti Nagar	1	8.69	13.83	3.3	17	0.42	0.94	1.74	0.33	1.62	3.22	0.48	0.19
Ravi Nagar	6.7	7.05	15.71	3.02	24	0.21	0.96	2.21	0.21	1.51	3.45	0.59	0.19
Nagpur	1	23.94	56.27	3.13	54	0.21	0.55	6.89	0.21	1.58	6.89	0.1	0.02

5.4 Select localities: Mahal and Trimurti Nagar

Mahal is the old part of Nagpur. It has organically evolved built environment. It is now the core of the city and is having mixed land-use throughout. Earlier it was having sub-localities based on occupation, having combined workplaces and residences. There are some retail and wholesale shops mostly on ground floor and residences on upper floors. The high-income business families have mostly moved out of the locality. Now it has middle-income households involved in retail business or lower income labour class. The Google image of the close-knit organic configuration of the built environment in Mahal is shown in Figs. 5.15 and 5.16. Unlike new parts of the city, it is a high density area with very little number of defined open spaces to be used as community spaces. Mostly the roads act as important social spaces. Many social activities, festive celebrations happen on roads, and one can experience a very intense social life in this area. The overall experience of this locality is intense, happening and humane.

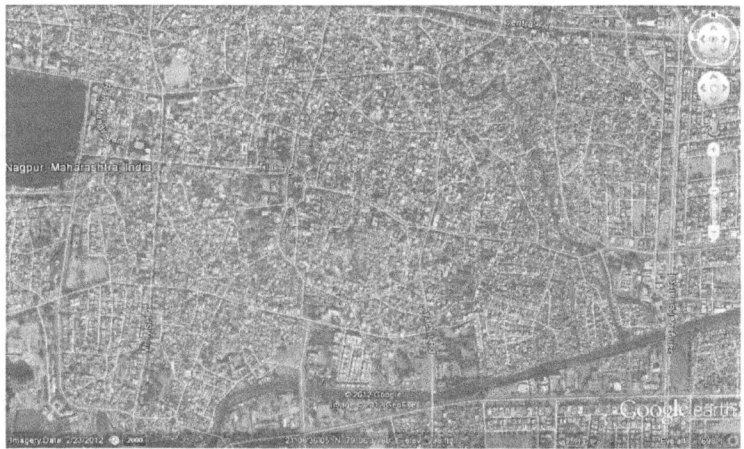

Figure 5.15 Google image: Mahal

Trimurti Nagar is developed in the last 25 years. It has mostly the planned development with grid-iron pattern. The working class people employed in public or private sector belonging mostly to middle-income group reside in this locality. There are few pockets of lower middle class or higher middle class. Most of the population is well educated and employed in government or private sector. Being planned development mostly through layouts by NIT, it has number of defined community spaces and parks. The most famous is Rajiv Gandhi Udyan or NIT Garden. Part of Ring Road passes through the middle of the locality and cuts the locality into two distinct parts.

Figure 5.16 Close knit, organically evolved urban fabric in Mahal

There are some urban villages like Bhamti and Parsodi which have now become integrated part of the urban fabric. Some of the unauthorized layouts listed in 572 and 1900 layouts are also part of this locality. The nature of the plotted development and the grid-iron pattern of configuration are seen in the Google images of Trimurti Nagar shown in Figs. 5.17 and 5.18.

Figure 5.17 Google image: Trimurti Nagar

Figure 5.18 Grid-iron pattern of Trimurti Nagar

5.5 Methodology

Cognitive constructs as user preferences in case of contemporary urban built environments are understood through a study of relationship between spatial configurations of built environments and spatial cognition of its users. Spatial configuration and cognition are studied in select urban built environments in a select developing city in India, namely Nagpur. The specific framework for this analysis is as follows:

Correlation study Cognition (Primary survey) Frequency of recognition and reasons for recognition Frequency of use of nodes and paths and reasons for it	Configuration (Syntactic analysis) Global integration, local integration, connectivity

How to deduce user preferences through study of relationship between spatial configurations of built environments and spatial cognition of its users?

Causal comparative study (Qualitative analysis)
1. Variations in spatial configuration, syntactic parameters and index of use of local and global facilities
2. Variations in spatial configuration, physical characteristics of buildings and index of recognition of landmarks/nodes/paths

First part is correlations study: The relationship between the variables is studied as significant associations through quantitative analysis. Also the reason for use of particular facility/ space and reason for recognition are quantified.

Second part is the causal comparative study: Indices of use and recognition are calculated to understand the combined effect of configuration on cognition. Based on the literature review and the identified research strategies, following matrix of concepts, indicators and methods is prepared.

Table 5.3 Matrix of parameters and methods

Variables	Parameters		Methods of data collection	Unit of analysis
Objective morphology/ Spatial configuration	Relational properties	Syntactic Properties: Global & local Integration	Syntactic analysis: Axial line modelling	Axial line
		Connectivity	Syntactic analysis: Axial line modelling	Axial line
		Synergy	Syntactic analysis: Axial line modelling	Axial line
		Intelligibility	Syntactic analysis: Axial line modelling	Axial line
	Discrete properties	Locations of landmarks, paths, nodes	Syntactic analysis: Axial line modelling	Axial lines on which landmarks are located
Subjective morphology/ Spatial cognition	Discrete elements Paths	Frequency of use Frequency of recognition and role of physical characteristics in recognition	Behaviour maps and recognition test Questionnaire for knowing reasons of use and recognition	Individual respondent
	Landmarks	Frequency of use / recognition and role of architectural characteristics in recognition	Recognition test Questionnaire for knowing reasons of use and recognition	Individual respondent
	Nodes	Frequency of use	Behaviour maps	Individual respondent
	Relational	Reasons for use and time of use	Questionnaire	Individual respondent
Personal aspects		Socioeconomic parameters/ familiarity and mode of travel, type of employment, workplace location	Questionnaire	Individual respondent

For the study of spatial cognition as a dependent of spatial configuration, a primary survey about the cognitive aspects is conducted. A standardized method of questionnaire survey was adopted (Annexure I). First the objectives of collecting data were sorted. It included data collection about socio-demographic, economic data about respondents, anthropological aspect of cognition through spatial behaviour, psychological aspect of cognition through recognition and reasons for recognition. Thus the questionnaire consists of four parts. First part of questionnaire is designed for socio-demographic characteristics and to externalize the anthropological aspect of cognition. In the questionnaire, respondents were asked about the places within the locality and outside the locality they visit for daily needs, garments shopping, electronic goods shopping, playing, walking, social gatherings, schools, colleges and health facilities. Also, questions such as the estimated distance of the facilities, time of visit and reason for visiting that specific place were asked. For finding use of activity nodes, facilities are divided into two categories: local and global. Local nodes are the ones within the delineated locality, and global are the ones which are outside the delineated locality.

Second part is recognition test, third part is post-experimental questionnaire for reasons of recognition and fourth part is behaviour map. Some of the cognitive, expressive and perceptual information about respondents' physical surroundings may be better expressed visually than verbally, through non-precoded techniques, such as maps and photographs (Zeisel, 1984, p.170). Sketch map and subjective distance assessment are well-accepted methods to externalize cognitive map. A pilot survey included sketch map activity and also subjective distance assessment. For understanding cognitive responses in pilot survey, a sketch map activity was done wherein a part plan of their locality with references in terms of important road, north and important landmarks was given (Long and Yixiang, 2007, p.100). The respondents were given time to mark their house location and other important landmarks, paths which are part of their routine life. The subjective distance of important institutional, commercial and recreational activities is assessed by respondents by ratio, interval and ordinal scaling. Both the methods, sketch maps and subjective distance assessment, are found to be inappropriate in case of Indian respondents. Hence, a recognition test based on photographic information is worked out. The landmarks shown in recognition tests are also categorized in terms of local and global. Local landmarks are referred to those which are within the locality, and global landmarks are those which are outside the locality. For such a test, important landmarks, nodes and paths located on axial lines with highest and second highest values of local/ global integration, in each locality, are identified. The photographs of these landmarks, paths and nodes were clicked at eye level in almost the same viewing angle as they are seen while moving on the road. The photographs at these identified locations are then printed on photo paper, and respondents are asked to recognize and mention the locations of the photographs. Such a task is done for local-level landmarks, nodes and paths, and also for global-level landmarks, nodes and paths. Third part of the questionnaire is post-recognition activity questionnaire, to assess the reasons for recognition. The questions are asked about the reasons for recognition of paths, landmarks, nodes and architectural aspects responsible for recognition and remembrance.

Behaviour map is another technique to externalize cognitive map of users; it has been used in this study. Here a Xeroxed map of the locality with north, all road network, important landmarks, water bodies if any, and open spaces is given to respondents. They are asked to mark their own residence, important roads, facilities and activity nodes they use routinely. This is the fourth part.

Data are collected for a set of random samples. The samples were from working age group who go daily out for work and other activities.

The configuration is quantified by syntactic analysis. The syntactic parameters such as local and global integration, connectivity of the activity nodes mentioned by respondents and the landmarks for recognition tests are noted from the axial line modelling. The parameters of the axial line on which the activity node or landmark is situated are considered as syntactic parameters of the activity node or landmark.

5.6 Observations and analysis

These socioeconomic characteristics of respondents of select localities such as education, work place location, employment, mode of travel and economic class, etc., are compared. Most of the characteristics are found homogeneous except education, work place location and employment. In the new locality, the respondents are of service class, more educated and have far-off work places, as compared to old locality.

The psychological aspect of cognition is externalized using the recognition test.

Frequency of use of paths and activity nodes are the parameters of cognition in terms of anthropological aspect. It is about user preferences. Frequency of recognition of landmarks is a parameter of cognition in terms of psychological aspect. The syntactic parameters such as connectivity, R3 and Rn are parameters of configuration. To understand the role of configuration in development of these two aspects of cognition, co-relationships between syntactic parameters and parameters of spatial cognition are studied. For studying the relationship, correlation coefficients between syntactic parameters such as R3, Rn, connectivity and frequency of use, frequency of recognition are calculated.

5.6.1 Cognition: Anthropological aspect

Table 5.4 Correlation Matrix: Syntactic parameters and frequency of use

New planned locality – Trimurti Nagar: Use of paths within the locality				
	R3	Rn	Connectivity	Frequency of use
R3	1			
Rn	0.82	1		
Connectivity	0.7	0.41	1	
Frequency of use	0.51	0.54	0.3	1

Contd...

Contd...

Old locality – Mahal: Use of paths within the locality

	R3	Rn	Connectivity	Frequency of use
R3	I			
Rn	0.77	I		
Connectivity	0.82	0.7	I	
Frequency of use	0.5	0.37	0.62	I

New planned locality – Trimurti Nagar: Use of activity nodes within the locality

	R3	Rn	Connectivity	Frequency of use
R3	I			
Rn	0.72	I		
Connectivity	0.46	0.74	I	
Frequency of use	0.31	0.70	0.46	I

Old locality – Mahal: Use of activity nodes within the locality

	R3	Rn	Connectivity	Frequency of use
R3	I			
Rn	0.69	I		
Connectivity	0.82	0.66	I	
Frequency of use	0.58	0.013	0.27	I

New planned locality – Trimurti Nagar: Use of activity nodes outside the locality

	R3	Rn	Connectivity	Frequency of use
R3	I			
Rn	-0.49	I		
Connectivity	0.87	0.083	I	
Frequency of use	0.0017	0.25	-0.13	I

Old locality – Mahal: Use of activity nodes outside the locality

	R3	Rn	Connectivity	Frequency of use
R3	I			
Rn	0.13	I		
Connectivity	0.84	0.22	I	
Frequency of use	0.35	0.13	0.53	I

To find out which syntactic parameter is affecting the relation significantly, t-Test for testing the significance of the sample correlation coefficients is carried out. It is found that if the local integration and global integration of a path are high, then more is the frequency of use of the road in Trimurti Nagar. However, in Trimurti Nagar area, there is no significant correlation between frequency of use and connectivity. For Mahal area, frequency of use of paths within the locality is positively correlated with R3 and connectivity, but there is no significant correlation between Rn and frequency of use.

If the local integration and connectivity of a path are high, then more is the frequency of use of the road in Mahal area. However, in Mahal area, there is no significant correlation between frequency of use and Rn. This means that good global integration does not contribute to the use of local roads. This establishes that residents of Mahal use locally integrated roads and subsequently local facilities more than the residents of Trimurti Nagar.

In new planned Trimurti Nagar locality, there is significant relationship with the global integration and frequency of use of activity nodes within the locality. Trimurti Nagar residents are more educated and are mostly employed in public/private sector. The workplace locations are outside the locality. Hence, may be because of the fact that residents of Trimurti Nagar have better commutability, they tend to use facilities located on global network.

In case of Mahal, the frequency of use of local activity nodes is significantly correlated to local integration. People tend to use facilities located on the local network rather than the global network. This is because of the configurational peculiarity where people tend to move on local network before getting connected to global network.

For use of activity nodes outside locality, none of the configurational parameters have any significant relationship for preferences about use of global activity nodes in case of Trimurti Nagar residents. In case of old locality Mahal residents, the preference about use of global activity nodes has significant correlation with connectivity. From the matrix, there is another observation that for activity nodes or paths in Mahal, there is a significant correlation among R3, Rn and connectivity. Similar configurational peculiarity is not observed for preferred paths or activity nodes at the city level, outside the locality. There is significant correlation between R3 and connectivity for the city-level activity nodes.

5.6.2 Cognition: Psychological aspect

Table 5.5 Correlation Matrix: Syntactic parameters and frequency of recognition

New planned locality – Trimurti Nagar: Recognition of local landmarks/ paths				
	R3	Rn	Connectivity	Frequency of recognition
R3	1			
Rn	−0.18	1		
Connectivity	0.86	−0.29	1	
Frequency of recognition	0.14	0.05	0.03	1
Old locality – Mahal: Recognition of local landmarks/ paths				
	R3	Rn	Connectivity	Frequency of recognition
R3	1			
Rn	0.65	1		
Connectivity	0.89	0.41	1	
Frequency of recognition	−0.27	−0.14	−0.27	1
New planned locality – Trimurti Nagar: Recognition of global landmarks/ paths				
	R3	Rn	Connectivity	Frequency of recognition
R3	1			
Rn	0.47	1		
Connectivity	0.93	0.5	1	
Frequency of recognition	0.03	−0.12	−0.008	1
Frequency of recognition (excluding Deekshbhumi)	0.12	0.52	−0.008	1

Contd...

Contd...

Old locality – Mahal: Recognition of global landmarks/ paths

	R3	Rn	Connectivity	Frequency of recognition
R3	I			
Rn	0.019	I		
Connectivity	0.89	0.66	I	
Frequency of recognition	−0.04	0.32	−0.08	I

Trimurti Nagar residents have significant correlation between Rn and recognition of global landmarks.

That is obvious as Trimurti Nagar residents use more global facilities. Psychological aspect of cognition, i.e. frequency of recognition, does not have relationship with syntactic parameters. Hence, the analysis about the role of architectural characteristics in recognition is carried out and is discussed further.

5.6.3   Index of use

It is observed that the use of local facilities and global facilities is not homogeneous in old Mahal and new planned Trimurti Nagar localities. Also, the residents in Mahal and Trimurti Nagar localities do not use the local facilities and global facilities in the same manner. Therefore, for comparative study of the use of local facilities and global facilities by the residents of Mahal and Trimurti Nagar localities, there is a need to develop an index for the use of the facilities. Index is a type of composite measure that summarizes and rank orders several specific observations and represents more general dimension (Babbie, 2004). Hence, index of anthropological aspect of cognition is worked out in terms of index of use of facilities at local and global level. Index of recognition of local and global landmarks is worked out for psychological aspect of cognition.

Index: Local facility

Following steps are undertaken to calculate the index of use of local facility.

1. The distance is the primary indicator of 'local'. Lesser the distance, the facility becomes more local. Hence, the scores are assigned to the local facility according to the distance travelled.

Distance travelled for the local facility	Up to 0.5	Up to 1	Up to 2
Score assigned	3	2	1

2. Then average score of each facility is calculated by using the following formula:

Average score for each facility

$$= \frac{\sum(\text{Score}) \times (\text{No. of respondents using the facility})}{\text{Total no. of respondents}}$$

3. Another important criterion for facility to be called as local is frequency of use in a month and number of respondents using the facility. Hence, weights to each of the local facility are assigned on the likely use of the facility and how many respondents use the facility out of the total number of respondents. Weights are the numbers that measure the importance of the facility. It is therefore natural to decide the weights on the basis of frequency of use and the proportion of total respondents using the facility. As per the frequency of the use of the facility in a month, following weights are assigned. For a facility used daily, i.e. at least 25 days a month, the proportion of days the facility is used in a month is 25/30. Hence the weight assigned is 25/30 = 0.8333. For a facility used weekly, i.e. at least four times a month, the proportion of days the facility is used in a month 4/30. Hence the weight assigned is 4/30 = 0.1333. For a facility used occasionally, i.e. at least once a month, the proportion of days the facility is used is 1/30. Hence the weight assigned is 1/30 = 0.0333. The proportion of respondents who use the

facility out of the total number of respondents can be calculated as follows. For example, 41 respondents out of 54 sampled respondents in Mahal use local facility for shopping of daily needs. Therefore, the proportion of respondents who use the local facility for shopping of daily needs = 41/54 = 0.759259259. The weight for each facility = (Proportion of days the facility is used in a month) × (Proportion of total respondents using the facility)

4. The index of use of local facility can be calculated by using the following formula: Index of use of local facility

$$= \frac{\sum (\text{Weight assigned to the facility}) \times (\text{Average score of the facility})}{\text{Total weight}}$$

$$= \frac{\text{Total weighted score}}{\text{Total weight}}$$

Index: Global facilities

1. Similar process as the one followed for index of use of local facility; is followed for calculation of index of use of global facility. The distance criteria for assigning the scores to facilities are different for global facility. The scores to the global facility according to the distance travelled are assigned as follows:

Distance travelled for the global facility	More than 2 km and any time visit up to 4 km	More than 4 km and up to 6 km	More than 6 km	
Score assigned	1	1	2	3	3

2. The average scores are calculated by using the following formula:

Average score for each facility

$$= \frac{\sum (\text{Score}) \times (\text{No. of respondents using the facility})}{\text{Total no. of respondents}}$$

Table 5.6 Indices of use of global and local facilities

Index of use on 3-point scale	Old Mahal	New planned Trimurti Nagar
Local facility	2.082	1.683
Global facility	1.276	2.254

These indices are quantitative indicators of the preference of use of facilities by the users. Thus, it can be seen that for old Mahal locality, index of use of local facility is more than the index of use of global facility. In new planned Trimurti Nagar locality, index of use of local facility is less than the index of use of global facility. That means the residents of Mahal locality prefer to use local facilities more than global facilities. Trimurti Nagar residents use global facilities more than local facilities, as index of use of global facilities in Trimurti Nagar is more than the index of use of global facilities by residents of Mahal. These indices give collective idea about the preferences of use of facilities by the users. Certainly there are differences in the preferences of users of the two select localities. The role of spatial configuration in deciding these preferences is discussed further.

5.6.4 Index of recognition

Recognition tests for local and global landmarks are carried out among the sampled residents of both the localities. The index of recognition is calculated to understand if psychological aspect of cognition has any role to play in the development of anthropological aspect of cognition, i.e. spatial behaviour /usage of spaces. The procedure of developing an index of the performance in recognition test is explained in the following steps.

1. Every landmark is evaluated from an architect's point of view on the characteristics of distinctiveness, function, historic importance and maintenance. Each landmark is assigned a score of either 0 or 1. These scores are used to calculate total score for each local as well as global landmark.
2. Using the frequency of recognition out of the total number of respondents, the proportion of respondents who recognize the landmark is calculated. These proportions are considered

as the weights for calculating the index of recognition by using the following formula:

Index of recognition

$$= \frac{\sum (\text{Weight assigned to the landmark}) \times (\text{Score assigned to the landmark})}{\text{Total weight}}$$

$$= \frac{\text{Total weighted score}}{\text{Total weight}}$$

Table 5.7 Indices of recognition

Index of recognition on a 4-point scale	Old locality Mahal	New planned locality Trimurti Nagar
For local landmarks	2.291	1.971
For global landmarks	2.326	2.327

In Mahal, the index of recognition for local landmarks is higher than that in case of Trimurti Nagar, and secondly it is approximately same as that of the global landmarks. In Trimurti Nagar, the index of recognition for global landmarks is greater than that of the local landmarks. It can be inferred from above indices that on a 4-point scale, the values of indices of recognition are moderate for local as well as global landmarks for both the localities. This indicates that lay persons are not much aware and observant about the visual appeal of the built forms around. Even in the informal discussions with the respondents, most of them confess their ignorance about the visual character of buildings they pass by daily.

This finding again validates our earlier finding that the residents of Mahal area use local facilities often. The residents of Trimurti Nagar area use global facilities to a greater extent than local; because it is natural to expect that the respondents recognize the landmarks in the area they frequently visit.

5.6.5 Architectural characteristics

It is observed through correlation study between frequency of recognition and syntactic parameters that there is no role played by configuration in recognition. Hence, there is a need to find out if building characteristics play any role in recognition. There are the reasons mentioned by respondents for recognition of landmarks. To understand if there is any relationship between the characteristics of a landmark and its recognition, following analytical study is done. The landmarks are evaluated and scores are given for the characteristics such as distinctiveness, function, historic importance and maintenance. These have emerged as prominent reasons by respondents for recognition of particular landmarks. The score is 1 if the landmark possesses the characteristic and 0 if the landmark does not possesses the characteristic. To find out which characteristics of landmarks influence recognition, point Bi-serial correlation coefficient between the frequency of recognition and the characteristic of the landmarks is used.

The sample correlation coefficient between recognition of local landmarks and distinctiveness in terms of height, colour, size, building elements for new planned Trimurti Nagar is significant. The sample correlation coefficient between recognition of global landmarks and distinctiveness in terms of height, colour, size, building elements for old locality Mahal is significant. The sample correlation coefficient between recognition of global landmarks and historic importance for new planned Trimurti Nagar seemed to be significant but not found so after the test.

There was an open-ended question in the post-experimental interview which asked respondents to mention the name of the building which they feel as the most appealing building in the locality. There were varied answers to this question. Respondents in Trimurti Nagar locality mentioned about corporate office buildings that have come up in IT Park. Some of them mentioned residences or flat schemes in the locality (Fig. 6.35). The questions such as "why they feel that as appealing building" were also asked. Most of them mentioned about its distinctive character in terms of height, colour, size, building elements and maintenance. Most of them are impressed with the use of bright colours, different forms and recent trends of use of glass, aluminium panelling in exteriors.

In case of Mahal, most of the respondents mentioned the most appealing building such as Empress Mall, Rajwada Palace and Laddu Gopal Building. Some of them even mentioned about some of the newly constructed private residences or flat schemes.

Very few talked about the old temples in the locality which were built in Bhosala period, or gates like Gandhi gate (Fig. 5.19). Couple of person talked about colonial buildings. It is realized that for common people, the important factor for any building to be appealing is its distinctiveness, maintenance and flashy appearance. While cognizing the buildings around, people hardly acknowledge the importance of building performance in terms of functionality, climate responsiveness or historic importance.

Figure 5.19 'Appealing buildings' mentioned by the respondents in new planned area (Trimurti Nagar)

5.7 Configurational peculiarity and user preferences

From the analytical studies of the cognitive responses about spatial behaviour in relation to spatial configuration, user preferences about use of spaces and roads are inferred.

Figure 5.20 'Appealing buildings' mentioned by the respondents in Mahal

- Though the respondent groups from two select localities are homogeneous with respect to socio-demographic characteristics such as age, gender and family size, there is a difference in the sampled respondents of the two localities with respect to education, workplace location and employment. In case of old locality Mahal, respondents' education level is lesser than respondents from Trimurti Nagar. They are mostly self-employed and their workplace is also situated in the same locality. In case of new planned Trimurti Nagar, residents are mostly well educated and are employed in public or private sector. Hence, their workplaces are distributed to far-off places throughout Nagpur. Mainly due to nature of employment and location of workplace, the commutability of the respondents from Trimurti Nagar is higher.

- For overall usage of the facilities at local or global level, it is seen that for old Mahal locality, index of use of local facilities is higher than the index of use of global facilities. The use of facilities at the local level is significant. For new planned Trimurti Nagar locality, index of use of local facilities is less than the index of use of global facilities. Also, use of local facilities for Trimurti Nagar is less than index of use of local facilities for Mahal locality. This indicates that the residents of Trimurti Nagar use global facilities to a greater extent than local. More use of local facilities by residents is not only sustainable but also enhances the chances of incidental encounters encouraging social interaction and cohesion.

- One of the reasons for this difference is commutability in case of new planned Trimurti Nagar residents. As they move longer distances throughout the city, they use global facilities more. Another reason is configurational peculiarity in case of Trimurti Nagar. The syntactic properties of the two select localities are discussed. In old locality Mahal, there are many small axes (Fig. 5.21). The axes in Trimurti Nagar are longer and fewer (Fig. 5.22). Though the average values of local and global integration are almost same in case of Mahal, there is significant variation in maximum and minimum values. Also the average values of connectivity are almost similar but in case of Mahal, there are few axes with very high connectivity. As far as synergy and intelligibility are concerned, there is not much difference but still old locality Mahal is more synergistic and less intelligible as compared to new planned Trimurti Nagar. Due to these syntactic peculiarities, the natural movement pattern in Mahal is more restricted to movement within the locality. It encourages the use of local facilities more and subsequently the social interaction and cohesion, making the locality much more humane. In case of new planned Trimurti Nagar locality, the syntactic configuration is

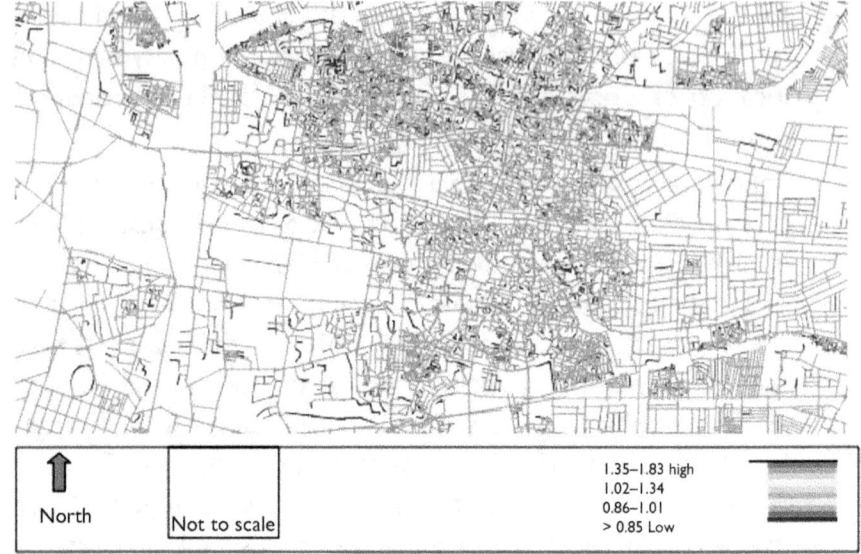

Figure 5.21 Global integration (Rn) map of Mahal: Smaller but many axes

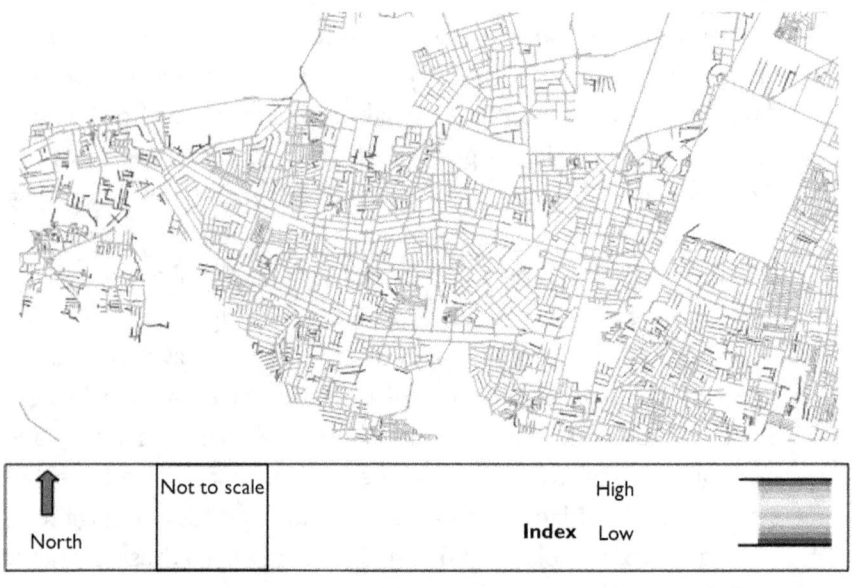

Figure 5.22 Global integration (Rn) map of Trimurti Nagar:
Longer and fewer axes

such that the natural movement pattern encourages movement on longer paths with higher global integration, leading to more use of global facilities than local. Thus, due to the configurational peculiarity in terms of longer and fewer axes with higher global integration, people in Trimurti Nagar tend to use global facilities more. The paths with higher Rn are also used more.

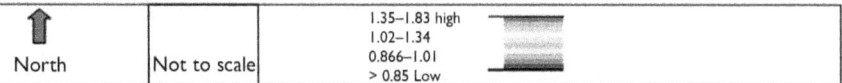

Figure 5.23 Local integration map of Mahal

Figure 5.24 Local integration map of Trimurti Nagar

- Local integration plans of the two localities are shown in Figs. 5.24 and 5.25. Variations in maximum and minimum values of local integration in case of old locality Mahal help in making residential streets physically segregated from the total system. Spatially segregated internal streets in Mahal, conducive for social activities, are shown in Fig. 5.25. This restricts the vehicular movement within streets encouraging their use as active social space. In case of new planned Trimurti Nagar, mostly due to grid-iron pattern, such variation does not exist. Many internal residential streets are equally physically integrated thus restricting their use as social spaces for playing or other activities such as celebration of festivals like Ganesh pooja. As shown in Fig. 5.26, there are many defined open spaces but they have restricted entry. Also these spaces are not as physically and visually integrated in the built fabric as the streets in Mahal are and hence less used.

- In Trimurti Nagar, there are more spaces with higher values of global integration. This is responsible for making the locality more intelligible. Yet, many of its axes are having less local

Figure 5.25 Social activities on internal streets of Mahal

Figure 5.26 Defined open spaces in Trimurti Nagar

integration. Thus, making the locality less synergistic compared to Mahal. In case of Mahal, though it is less intelligible, it is more synergistic and spaces within system are not directly connected to global system but they have a hierarchy, and spaces at local level gradually get connected to spaces at global level. This also helps in use of local facilities as you are confronted with local facilities before you get connected with global system.

- To understand further how user preferences as cognitive constructs are related to configuration, two sub-localities in Trimurti Nagar are selected. One is Gopal Nagar which has mostly evolved from urban villages called Bhamti, Parsodi and another is Saraswati Vihar. These two are selected as they have some peculiarity in terms of non-congruence between planning and imposed order by users.

In case of Gopal Nagar, the complete area including the main road is demarcated with proposed land use as residential, as per 2001

Figure 5.27 Local integration map and immergence of activity node: Gopal Nagar

development plan. However, in the last decade, the main road has transformed into a market street and is flooded with retail shops of vegetable, grocery, daily needs and even specific products like garments, electronic goods and pharmaceuticals. Initially it was only a local market for Gopal Nagar residents only but now residents from other sub-localities even sometimes visit the market for daily needs. Trimurti Nagar in general has a different configuration than Mahal. Within Trimurti Nagar, Gopal Nagar has a configurational peculiarity and has given the area a Mahal kind of appearance. Here as shown in Fig. 5.27, the local main street has highest local integration and all smaller residential streets join to the middle local street, before getting connected to global network. This has led to development of a retail market on the street and eventually that street has become an important social space and hub for some social events and celebrations (Fig. 5.27).

Instead, in another sub-locality called Saraswati Vihar, the road in the residential area is planned with commercial land use. It was required for the residents to have shutters for shops in their front façade (Fig. 5.28). In last decade, the shops were opened on the street but due to lack of business the shops gradually shut down. Residents have converted the front shutter space into living spaces. It is a street with very low local integration. Thus, even planned as commercial, due to configurational peculiarity, the street has not developed into one.

Note to scale
North
Street with proposed commerical landuse in Saraswati Vihar

Figure 5.28 Local integration map of Saraswati Vihar

Hence, when the planning decisions are to be made, it is important to understand preferences about space proxemics. This may help in reducing the conflicting situations in emerging built environments in urban India that arise due to non-congruence between planning and user preferences.

5.8 Summary

It can be finally concluded that due to socio-demographic and economic peculiarity of the situation, Indian society has different way of thinking. Indian society is polychronic in nature where people tend to do multiple tasks at a time. Hence, the user preferences are based on the subjective norms of convenience. Physical and visual linkages through configuration play an important role in deciding the user preferences about movement and use of facilities in built environment. These preferences though not guided by configuration at larger city level but at local level are certainly affected by configuration. The use of local paths and facilities in a particular manner not only is good from sustainability point of view but also boosts social interactions at local level. It may be stated that more use of local facilities will help in improving social cohesion and social environment.

It is important to understand user preferences as cognitive constructs about the use of spaces for various formal, informal activities and their configurational peculiarities. This culture-specific use of spaces, i.e. space proxemics, will help us to better understand our built environments the way they evolve and the way they need to be dealt.

5.9   References

- Babbie, E. R. (2004). *The Practice of Social Research*. Belmont: Cengage Learning.
- Long, Y. (2007). *The Relationships Between Objective and Subjective Evaluations of the Urban Environment: Space Syntax, Cognitive Maps, and Urban Legibility* (Unpublished Doctoral work) North Carolina State University, Raleigh, North Carolina
- Nagpur Improvement Trust (2011). *City Development Plan , Nagpur*. Nagpur. Retrieved from April 22, 2011 http://www.nitnagpur.org/dp.html#masterplan
- Shah, D. (n.d.). Manifestations for a City [HONOURABLE MENTION] | Resilient City. Retrieved November 10, 2012, from http://www.resilientcity.org/index.cfm?PAGEPATH=Competition/Manifestations_for_a_City__HONOURABLE_MENTION_&ID=23091
- Zeisel, J. (1984). *Inquiry by Design: Tools for Environment-Behaviour Research*. Cambridge: Cambridge University Press.

Chapter 6

Chapter 6

Principles of urbanism for Indian cities

Abstract: Based on the theoretical and analytical studies discussed earlier, this chapter summarizes the principles of urbanism peculiar in Indian cities. The contemporary approach for generating order in spatial configurations in architectural design or planning is also discussed. The culture-specific cognitive constructs as user preferences about use of space are certainly different than the current principles of urban planning adopted in Indian context which are based on British planning norms. Consideration of user preferences can help to reduce conflicting situations in urban areas due to non-congruence between planning principles adopted and principles of urbanism rooted in the place.

Key words: Organic developments, Euclidian geometry, concept of depth, topology, urbanism

6.1 Planning practices: Euclidian geometry

The concepts of spatial configuration, spatial cognition and evolution of spatial configurations through past, present and future are referred. The contemporary approach for generating order in spatial configurations in architectural design or planning is also looked upon, and it can be stated that the contemporary approach is based on Euclidian geometry. As designers and planners, we have started evolving designs/plans following an approach based on the geometry – cartography. Even the tools that are used for conception of spaces such as drawings, CAD or GIS, are also based on premise of cartography and Euclidian geometry. The investigation has tried to understand the way users impose order in urban situations which at times is not in congruence with the order generated by configuration derived out of Euclidian geometry. Hence, there is a need to move from a surveyor's conception of space and emphasize on user's perception and preferences. Instead of only relying on the cartography and principles of Euclidian geometry with its practical benefits, we as planners and designers need to go beyond and think about deriving configurations based on the understanding or the way users impose order. It needs to emphasize the topology of spaces rather than geometry.

The spatial configuration of organically evolved traditional built environments is studied to understand the culture-specific user preferences rooted in it. It highlighted that organic development is never an uncontrolled and unplanned development but rather it results out of many decisions based on cognitive constructs as culture-specific user preferences of space proxemics. Visual order is usually given importance when principles from traditional settlements are extrapolated to present context in the planned developments. In organic settlements, it is the irregular geometry with shifting axis and element of surprise is given importance. However, organic cities are not about visual order. They adapt to individual, social and economic preferences, to the constraints of the natural landscape, and to the dominant technology of the city (Batty and Longley, 1994, pp. 28–31). The pattern of hierarchies along with the fine variations in the depth evolves not out of imposed geometrical order but it involves continuous process of making many decisions at many stages. Thus traditional urbanism is in fact intensely interactive, computational and adaptive where the set of rules are not always predetermined and unchangeable, but they evolve along with the built environment.

This does not mean to let the organic development happen. Orthogonality, Euclidian geometry will certainly have to play a role in the emergence of built environments, but there is a need to go beyond with emphasis on topology, hierarchy and culture-specific user preferences of space proxemics. It demands a fresh approach to look at designing and planning built environments. The decision making has to be much more adaptive, flexible, continuing and non-simplistic... like organic developments. Also the evolved configurations should have topologies having required kind of hierarchies relating to culture-specific user preferences of space proxemics.

6.2   Principles of urbanism

The principles of urbanism are understood from the analytical studies presented earlier. These principles of urbanism may not be similar in all Indian cities, but investigation has shown that there are such culture-specific norms, and secondly there are some commonalities. The study of relationship of spatial cognition and spatial configuration has helped to deduce following principles of urbanism.

1. *Depth in terms of number of steps plays an important role in use of spaces and also emergence of social spaces.* Configurations either provide for or restrict movement pattern leading to unintended social interactions and subsequently development of certain social cohesion (Fig. 6.1).
2. *Accessibility in terms of physical and visual linkages is governed by configuration.* Due to socioeconomic and demographic peculiarities of Indian society, accessibility is viewed in a peculiar way in terms of time, money and convenience. Also Indian society by and large is polychronic in nature, which means Indians prefer to do many tasks at a time. Hence, the westernized planning and design approach based on zoning and spatial segregation does not work much. *Users mostly prefer the use of facilities which are accessible as they move for work or activities* (Fig. 6.2).

Figure 6.1 Evolved social space

Figure 6.2 Commercial developments on highly accessible movement corridors

3. *Unlike at the larger city level, at local/neighbourhood level, preferences about use of paths or activity nodes are more affected by configuration.* There are other aspects such as quality and cost which play an important role in deciding user preferences at city level. Hence, we as designers and planners need to take into consideration the cognitive constructs as user preferences for dealing especially urban neighbourhoods (Fig. 6.3).

Figure 6.3 Urban neighbourhood

4. *In India medium-size developing cities, streets have been and still continue to be important social spaces than the defined open spaces* (Fig. 6.4). *In demand of higher visibility, streets are used often in spite of availability of defined open spaces. Variety of social, political, recreational, commercial, religious activities, festive celebrations happen on the streets. Social use of streets also affects the social interactions. Topological relationships in terms of depth distances affect the hierarchy of streets and their uses for variety of social activities.*

Figure 6.4 Streets as social space

Streets with high local integration, i.e. streets with high accessibility, are used for retail commercial and processions. They emerge as local activity nodes. Streets with medium integration are used for informal shopping and community festive celebrations. The temporary structures erected for community festivals are usually on these streets so that they have direct physical and visual linkage with street having high local integration. Internal streets in residential areas with high depth and low integration are used for small family functions, marriage parties, community get-togethers, recreational activities such as playing cricket, etc.

The use of street for social activities certainly affects the traffic and creates conflicting situation. This does not mean we need to encourage or totally discourage it. However, while dealing Indian built environments, there is a need to take cognizance of the topological relationships of streets. On the basis of where we want to encourage and where we want to discourage the use of street for social activities, the spatial configurations of built environments can be worked out. If any kind of social activities are expected on streets, then it necessitates proper physical design of streets so as to avoid conflicting situations.

Figure 6.5 Visibility of facilities

5. *The user preference is not only for physically accessible but also for visible facilities* (Fig. 6.5). This is an inherent peculiarity of Indian society due to cultural background and is generally ignored while designing built environments. This is very much different than developed societies like American which apparently give more attention towards content rather than visible structure or form. For many activities, where quality and cost are not the

criteria for deciding preferences, it is neither metric distance nor geometry of road network that governs the preferences; but in such cases, configurational/topological relationships play much more significant role in deciding preferences.

The culture-specific cognitive constructs as user preferences about use of spaces are certainly different than the current principles of urban planning adopted in Indian context which are based on British planning norms. Consideration of user preferences can help to reduce conflicting situations such as illegal encroachments, communal conflicts and environmental hazards happening in urban areas due to non-congruence between planning principles adopted and principles of urbanism rooted in the place.

6.3 References

- Batty, M., and Longley, P. (1994). *Fractal Cities: A Geometry of Form and Function*. London: Academic Press.

Chapter 7

Chapter 7

Humane approach for planning practices

Abstract: The chapter summarizes the humane approach for planning practices. There are some profound understandings which planners and designers need to consider. User cognizes and then uses built environments primarily according to topological relationships, yet the method adopted for evolution of built environments through planning and design is primarily concerned with geometry and not topology. Spatial modelling to incorporate the humane approach is also discussed.

Key words: Spatial modelling, planning practices, humane approach, topology, geometry

7.1 Humane approach

Humane approach for dealing built environments can be considered by the following points, which have emerged from the analytical studies described in earlier chapters.

- *Design is predominantly a configurational activity.* Designing built environment should not only be the result of individual creative intuition, but also be based on collective knowledge of users, society and its interface with built environment.
- *Configurational analysis provides us the accessibility, but the way accessibility is envisioned by the users depends upon the common cognitive constructs due to socio-economic peculiarities of the Indian society.*
- *User cognizes and then uses built environments primarily according to topological relationships.* Distinctive architecture, geometry or metric distances have limited role in spatial cognition and subsequent spatial behaviour.
- *Hence, in case of orthogonally planned or organically evolved built environments, it is not just geometry that is important to be discussed for analyzing or designing but topology is also equally important.* Geometry remaining same, topology may differ and vice versa.
- *In organically evolved settlements, there is a culture-specific role of the depth and hierarchy, which is getting lost in contemporary city planning and also in architecture.*
- The main differentiation between planned and organic city forms lies in the process of creating them. *The method adopted for evolution of built environments through planning and design is primarily concerned with geometry and not topology.* Spatial configuration in terms of topological relationships is significantly neglected in contemporary formal planning process/design process.
- For dealing built environments in urban India, spatial design approach based on interactive steps related to understanding of users' cognitive response can be of better assistance.

Based on the study of the interrelationship between spatial configuration and spatial cognition in Indian context, the principles of urbanism are stated. This understanding can help planners and designers while dealing emerging built environments in urban India. A spatial design approach is evolved with spatial modelling based on cognitive response.

7.2 Proposed spatial modelling

Spatial modelling use data such as rules, constraints from the site, brief, and planning legislation; a previously built example as a model; intuition, etc. to make a design decision. Thus in this investigation, spatial design refers to modelling of spatial configurations based on understanding of users' cognitive response. The conceptual approach for spatial modelling based on many interactive steps related to understanding of users' cognitive response is developed and shown in Fig. 7.1.

An algorithm is a procedure or formula for solving a problem. It is a set of rules that precisely defines the sequence of operations to arrive at desired results for a given problem. Salingros (2005) argued that we as designers should conceptualize urban design not as one fully formed vision, but as a computational process employing algorithms consisting of many interactive steps. The method adopted for its evolution should be based on topological modelling of spaces where interactive adaptive algorithm is used rather than conventional top-to-down planning approach with Euclidian geometry.

A built environment consists of elements and the grammar of its composition or configuration. It's like any language which consists of two parts: a catalogue of a given language's words which is called as a lexicon and a system of rules which allows for the combination of those words into meaningful sentences which is called as grammar. Due to the lexicons and grammar, it leads to a certain way of expression through language which is called as semantics. To understand about the elements, their configuration and semantics for a given built environment, the existing reality is to be modelled for spatial analysis.

The syntactic analysis can help to understand spatial configuration. Externalizing spatial cognition of its users through the study of spatial behaviour can help to understand user preferences of space proxemics. The study of correlation of spatial cognition of users'

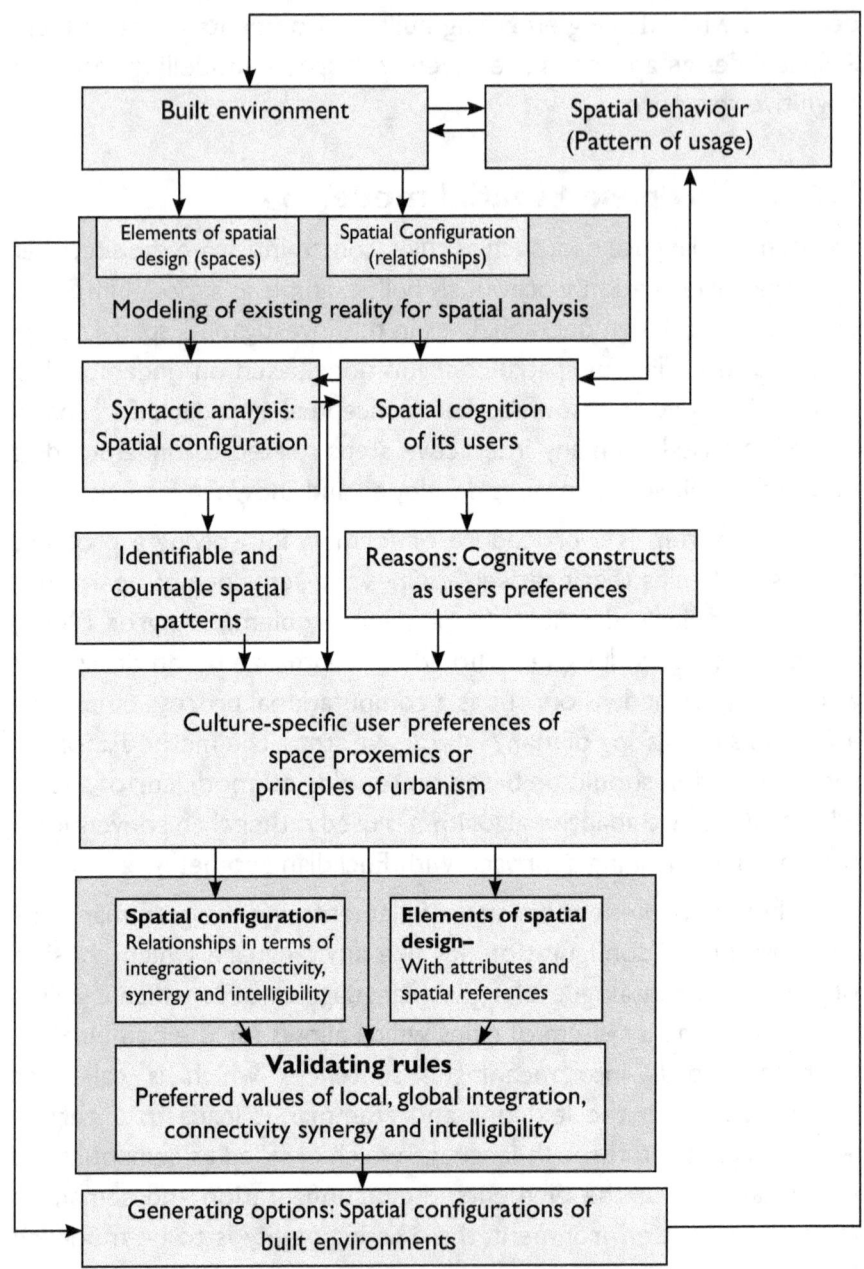

Figure 7.1 Proposed spatial modelling

of the built environment and its spatial configuration can help to deduce identifiable and countable patterns of spatial configuration and reasons in terms of user preferences. The understanding of culture-specific user preferences of space proxemics or principles of urbanism helps to derive validating rules in terms of desired configurational parameters, specific to a given built environment. The rules will be of preferred configuration in terms of values of syntactic parameters such as local and global integration, connectivity, synergy and intelligibility. The modelling of the elements can be done as they have attributes in terms of its use, dimensions, etc., and spatial references. The desired values of configuration parameters such as integration, connectivity, synergy and integration can be incorporated in the model along with the validating rules.

Thus, the spatial model generated can lead to evolve options in terms of possible configurations of built environment under consideration. These options can then be tested for their performance, and most appropriate option to be chosen for further detailing and implementation. Thus the design/planning process is much more objective, iterative, interactive and adaptive wherein options are generated, analyzed, checked against validating rules to arrive at the final solution.

7.3   Reforms for urban planning practices

The general plan process for dealing urban environments is summarized in Section 2.2 of Chapter 2. In contemporary planning practices, somewhere user preferences are not given due importance. Objectives/goals, policies/standards are framed and then designers and planners are primarily responsible for actions in terms of master plans, area plans and building plans. The cognitive approach to spatial modelling will help designers to know user preferences when they are either redeveloping any built environment or designing a totally afresh on a virgin site. As shown in Fig. 7.1, the study of relationship of spatial configuration and spatial cognition can help to decipher cognitive constructs as user preferences.

This understanding of user preferences can contribute for better understanding of existing situation and reasons behind it. Also it can help us in formulating appropriate planning goals or objectives. Innovative and relevant method of spatial design can be developed as

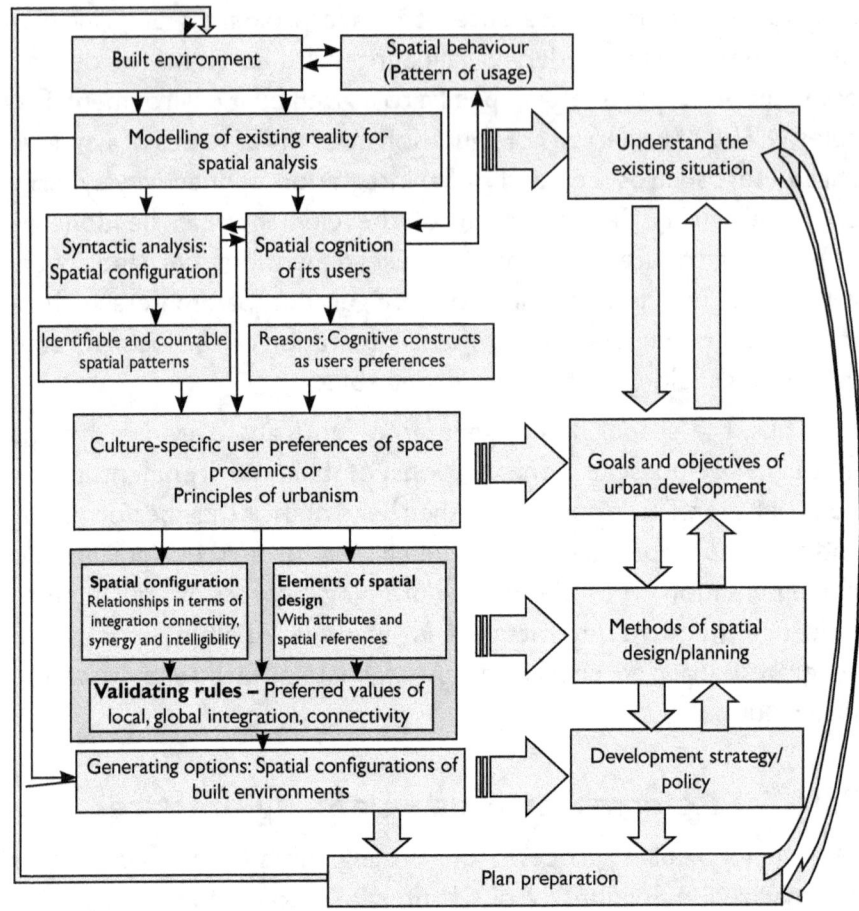

Figure 7.2 Applicability in general plan process

against the current planning practices adopted to deal contemporary built environments in urban India. This will aid in making plan process much more context specific and humane, as it will be in congruence with culture-specific user preferences. Taking a specific urban situation, studying the topology of configurational pattern, cognitive reasons and evolving a design/planning solution based on these is out of the scope of the investigation. Development of GIS-based programme for spatial modelling based on cognitive approach and syntactic analysis can be done but will need more investigation with predictive result. It can come under future scope of the investigation.

This applies universally to all instances of the built environment including a building, a campus, and a neighbourhood to a city. Neighbourhood is an area intermediate between the dwelling and the whole city. Thus, though it is a physical entity, basically it is a cognitive construct. Thus, a neighbourhood is the intermediate scale in a built environment which is quite crucial as far as configuration and its effects in terms of social behaviour are concerned. There is a need to maintain the coherent harmonious link among a house, a neighbourhood and a city, instead of developing into a fragmented urbanity (Valerio and Frederico, 2007). Hence, the urban neighbourhoods can be dealt with spatial design approach based on considerations of user preferences. Also, the complexity theorists advise that urban interventions are to be avoided at large urban scales and are to be carried out with extreme caution even at a small city scales (www.fractalmorphology.com, n.d.). The identified scale of built environment where interactions between space and its users have significance is neighbourhood. And for dealing urban neighbourhoods, the more appropriate approach is spatial design approach based on understanding of spatial cognition of users.

Thus, the process of design need not only be analytical synthesis but should be based on understanding of users. It should be generative, evaluative and predictive.

7.4 References

- Chapter 2: *The conventional Geometry of Straight Lines.* (n.d.). Retrieved November 8, 2012 from http://www.fractalmorphology.com/chapters/final%20Ch.2.pdf
- Valerio and Frederico (2007). *A Step Further: Segment Analysis for Comparative Urban Studies.* In Proceedings, 6th Space Syntax Symposium, Istanbul. Presented at the 6th International Space Syntax Symposium, Istanbul, Turkey. Retrieved November 26, 2011 from www.spacesyntaxistanbul.itu.edu.tr/papers%5Clongpapers%5C030%.
- Salingaros, N. (2005). *Principles of Urban Structure.* Amsterdam: Techne Press.

Index

A

Abstraction, 74
Architectural characteristics, 145–147
Axial lines
    depth and connectivity, 66
Axial map, 57
    graphic technique, 66
    modeling, 57–60
    spatial configuration, syntactic measures, 65
    syntactic measures, 66f–67f
    syntactic properties, 65–69

B

Baroque planning layout, 53
Behaviour map, 136
Bhopal
    built environments, 95–96, 96f
    global integration map, 103, 104f
Building design and its use, coherence between, 39
Built environment, 4–8
    and intense interactions between users, 8f
    and man relationship, 12–13
    anthropological aspect, 15
    anthropological sense,

cognition, 13
axial lines, 57
axial-line modeling, 57
cognition, anthropological view, 15
cognitive constructs, 13
configurational analysis, 170
depth, 55–69
design, knowledge base, 11
determinants, 6, 6f
humane approach, 170
humane aspects, 9
human response, importance and role, 34
interrelated characteristics, 45–46
investigation approach, 16f
node analysis, 56–57
physical configuration, 7
physical determinism, 50–51
social needs, 46–47
space syntax methodology, 55–56
spaces, 5
spatial cognition, 13–15
spatial configuration, 13–14
spatial experience, 12
syntactic analysis, 55
unbuilt spaces, 55
visual-field analysis, 56

C

Chandigarh
- global integration map, 106, 107f
- planned built environment, 101

Cities, 10, 11, 15, 16, 22, 23, 24, 27, 36, 44, 87, 93, 101, 112
- contemporary, 117
- cosmopolitan, 109
- design, 4
- developing, 33, 53, 94, 95, 117, 118, 119
- modern, 32, 39
- organic, 93, 112, 160
- planned, 53, 54,

Cognition for users, 35

Cognition
- socio-economic and cultural aspects, 75–78

Cognitive constructs, 15

Cognitive map, 71
- urban settings, 74–75

Cognitive mapping, 71
- common cultural background, 73–74
- configurational knowledge, 72–73
- direct communication with the physical environment, 74
- environmental information, structuring, 74
- relational knowledge, 72
- spatial knowledge, 72
- subjective distance, 73
- travel plans or spatial behavior, 73
- urban environment, subjective evaluation, 75

Community open spaces, 83

Community spaces, 61, 131

Configurational peculiarity, 127

Contemporary built environments, 10
- spatial configurations, 9

Contemporary cities, user preferences, 117–155

Convex spaces (urban open spaces), 55

Correlation matrix
- syntactic parameters and frequency of recognition, 140t–141t
- syntactic parameters and frequency of use, 137t–138t

Culture-specific
- meanings, 35
- user aspects, 4
- user preferences, 9, 160
- values, 9

Curved linear spaces, 58

Curved spaces, axial lines, 58f

D

Design user-centric built environments, 54

Districts, 37

E

Edges, 37
Electroencephalography (EEG), 70
Environment behavior, 42
    investigation, 34
Environment
    spatial configuration, 34
Environmental
    cognition, 70
    determinism, 35
    effects, 'filters' in the mind, 35
    perception, 70
    probabilism, 42
Euclidian geometry, 51–54, 86, 160–161, 171
Exploration, 16

F

Fractal geometries, 43

G

Geography, attitudes in, 34–35
Geometry, 43, 51, 52, 53, 86, 87, 93, 160, 166, 170
Geometry of spaces, 17, 41, 44, 93
Global facility, index of use, 143–144
Global integration, 59, 66, 67–68, 101, 102, 136, 139, 149–151, 152
Global landmarks, index of recognition, 136, 140, 141, 144–146

Good urban environment, performance dimensions, 38
Gopal Nagar, configurational peculiarity, 150
Graph theory, 58

H

Hierarchies, 53
Highly segregated interior residential streets, 113
Hippodamus, 52

I

Index of anthropological aspect of cognition, 141
Index of recognition, 144–145
Index of use, 141–144
India
    built environments, 4, 8, 60–69, 93–102
        applicability, 60–65
        axial-line modeling, 61
        cities, criteria for selection of samples, 94–95
        sample selection, 94
        street, 61
        syntactic properties, 65–69
    urban planning practices, 4
Indian cities, 4, 27, 82, 93, 108–109, 112, 113
    urbanism, 159–166
Indian history, 23–25
    Bombay Improvement Trust (BIT), 24

new value system, 24
Patrick Geddes 1920, 24
town planning acts, 24
town planning acts, 24–25
Integration of a line, 66
Intelligibility, 68

L

Landmarks, 37
Linear spaces (roads), 55
Local facility, index of use, 142–143
Local integration, 67–68
Local landmarks, Index of recognition, 136, 140, 145, 146
Lucknow
  built environments, 96–97, 97f
  global integration map, 105f, 106

M

Man–environment relationship, 34
Megalopolis, cognitive schemata, 36
Modern cities, structure of, 32
Modernist city planning practices, 33
Multilayered built environments, 7

N

Nagpur, 118–129
  built environments, 100–101, 10f
  causal comparative study, 134
    Chor bazar near Empress mall, configurational peculiarity, 127
  cognitive constructs as user preferences, 133–136
  configurational peculiarities and user behaviours, 123–129
  correlations study, 134
  global integration map, 102, 103f
  global integration values, 123
  Mahal, organically evolved built environment, 130–131, 131f, 132f
  parameters and methods, matrix, 134t
  settlement evolution, 119f
  socio-demographic characteristics, 129
  spatial configuration, 134–136
  syntactic analysis, 120–123
  syntactic properties, 129–130
  Trimurti Nagar, planned development with grid-iron pattern, 131, 132f, 133f
    vibrant social space, 128
Nashik
  built environments, 99, 99f
  global integration map, 104f, 105

Natural movement, 92
Neurophysics, 70–71
New planned Trimurti Nagar residents
   configurational peculiarity, 151
   commutability difference, 149
   open spaces, 151–153
   syntactic configuration, 149–150
Nodes, 37
Numerical synthesis
   central Indian cities, comparative analysis of syntactic parameters, 108f, 108–109
   number of axes and area, relationship between, 108f
   peripheral spaces, 109
   traditional settlements, integration values, 109

O

Objective morphology, 16
Old Mahal locality
   index of use for global vs local facilities, 149
Old Nagpur, system of spaces, 5
Open spaces, 57, 58, 127, 128, 131, 136, 152, 153, 164
Organic spatial configuration, 9
Organically evolved configuration, 54
Organically evolved settlements, 170

Orthogonally planned or organically evolved built environments, 170

P

Participatory planning paradigm, 27
Paths, 37
Permeability graphs, 58, 59f
Possibilism, 35
Premise, 15
Probabilism, 35
Proposed spatial modeling, 172f
Proximity, 49
Public participatory planning, 26–27

R

Radius3, 68
Residential apartment, 10
Respondents of select localities socioeconomic characteristics, 137

S

Segregated spaces, 102, 106
Social cohesion, 48
Social encounters, 48
Social order, 41
Social spaces, 84, 87, 113, 125, 127, 152, 161, 164
Socio-cultural factors, 34
Space (s), 51, 59, 60
   linear, 55, 58, 87
   non-linear organization, 60

pattern, 51
proxemics, 49–50, 54
syntax, 44–45, 55
systematizing, 7
topology, 41, 160
Spatial behavior, 17
Spatial cognition, 69–70
  development of, 35f
Spatial configuration
  past, present and future, 51–55
    grid, virtue, 53
    organic pattern, 51
    planned settlements, 52
    system of spaces, 44
    urban structure, 53
    and spatial cognition, 14f
    individual space, quality, 44
    traditional urban core (Varanasi), 92 92f
    value-formed attitudes, 47
Spatial knowledge/ knowledge of a place, 72–73, 76, 78
Spatial modeling, 171–173
    culture-specific user preferences, 173
    GIS-based programme, 174
    syntactic analysis, 171
Spatial organization, 6
Subjective morphology, 16
Synergy, 68
Synoecism, 6
Syntactic parameters
    traditional Indian built environments vs world scenario, 111–112, 111f, 112t
    traditional cities and Chandigarh, 110f
System of spaces, 5, 7, 13, 17, 41, 44, 45, 55, 57, 60, 61, 65, 67, 81, 91, 92, 93, 101–103, 105, 106

T

Theorists
  Amos Rapoport, 34–36
  Jane Jacobs, 33
  Lewis Mumford (1961), 32–33
Topography, 6
Topological graphs, 59
Topology, 17
Total depth (TD), 59
Traditional built environment, 68, 93
  geometrical properties, 93
  organically evolved parts of settlements, 93
Traditional Indian settlements
  configurational peculiarities, 113
Transformations, 39–40

U

Urban areas
  conflicting situation, 27f
Urban cores
  configuration parameters, 101
  space syntax methodology, 102

syntactic analysis, 102
Urban morphology, 13, 43, 45, 55
Urban planners
  Bill Hillier and Julienne Hanson, 40–41
  Christopher Alexander, 38–40
  Jane Jacobs, 42
  Kevin Lynch, 36–38
  Lewis Mumford, 42
Urban planning practices, 173–175
  urban neighbourhoods, spatial design approach, 175
  neighbourhood, 175
Urban planning principles, 9
Urban rationality, 4, 11
Urbanism, 22–23
  principles, 161–166
    number of steps, depth, 161, 162f
    physical and visual linkages, accessibility, 161, 162f
    streets, social use, 164, 164f
    streets, use for social integration, 165
    use of paths or activity nodes, configuration, 163, 163f
    visible facilities, user preference, 165–166

Urbanization, 4, 22
User preferences, 6, 9–11, 12–13, 15–17
  cognitive constructs, 36, 41–43, 74
  comprehension, 41–43
  culture-specific, 50, 88, 160, 174t
  in contemporary cities, 121–156
  space proxemics, 83–86, 161, 171, 172t, 173
  spatial design approach, urban neighbourhoods, 175
  and traditional Indian settlements, 91–113
  urban built environments, 54
  urbanization and urbanism in India, 25–27
  use of spaces and roads, 148–155
User–built environment relationship, 51f
User–space relationship, 41

V

Varanasi
  built environments, 98, 98f
  global integration map, 105, 106f
  number of axes, 108
  syntactic parameters, 109
  traditional urban core, 92
Visual order, 160

183

www.ingramcontent.com/pod-product-compliance
Lightning Source LLC
Chambersburg PA
CBHW051524230426
43668CB00012B/1730